3-MINUTE
Prayers
for Families

W9-BUP-018

© 2015 by Barbour Publishing, Inc.

Written by Shanna D. Gregor.

Print ISBN 978-1-63409-116-9

eBook Editions:
Adobe Digital Edition (.epub) 978-1-63409-118-3
Kindle and MobiPocket Edition (.prc) 978-1-63409-117-6

All rights reserved. No part of this publication may be reproduced or transmitted for commercial purposes, except for brief quotations in printed reviews, without written permission of the publisher.

Churches and other noncommercial interests may reproduce portions of this book without the express written permission of Barbour Publishing, provided that the text does not exceed 500 words and that the text is not material quoted from another publisher. When reproducing text from this book, include the following credit line: "From *3-Minute Prayers for Families*, published by Barbour Publishing, Inc. Used by permission."

Scripture quotations marked ESV are from The Holy Bible, English Standard Version®, copyright © 2001 by Crossway Bibles, a publishing ministry of Good News Publishers. Used by permission. All rights reserved.

Scripture quotations marked NCV are taken from the New Century Version of the Bible, copyright © 2005 by Thomas Nelson, Inc. Used by permission. All rights reserved.

Scripture quotations marked NKJV are taken from the New King James Version®. Copyright © 1982 by Thomas Nelson, Inc. Used by permission. All rights reserved.

Scripture quotations marked NLT are taken from the *Holy Bible*, New Living Translation, copyright © 1996, 2004, 2007 by Tyndale House Foundation. Used by permission of Tyndale House Publishers, Inc. Carol Stream, Illinois 60188. All rights reserved.

Scripture quotations marked AMP are taken from the Amplified® Bible, © 1954, 1958, 1962, 1964, 1965, 1987 by The Lockman Foundation. Used by permission.

Scripture quotations marked MSG are from *THE MESSAGE*. Copyright © by Eugene H. Peterson 1993, 1994, 1995, 1996, 2000, 2001, 2002. Used by permission of NavPress Publishing Group.

Published by Barbour Books, an imprint of Barbour Publishing, Inc., P.O. Box 719, Uhrichsville, Ohio 44683, www.barbourbooks.com

Our mission is to publish and distribute inspirational products offering exceptional value and biblical encouragement to the masses.

 Member of the
Evangelical Christian
Publishers Association

Printed in the United States of America.

3-MINUTE
Prayers
for Families

Shanna D. Gregor

BARBOUR BOOKS
An Imprint of Barbour Publishing, Inc.

Family is a God-idea and He purposely placed yours in your life. Each day serves as an opportunity to grow in faith together. Family should offer love, laughter, hope, and unconditional love, and home should be the one place where you feel safe and protected from the world.

Prayer is the first place to start—individually and as a family. God wants to talk to you and hear from you. He has a purpose and a plan for your family. God sent Jesus, His only Son, to give everyone the opportunity to become a part of His family: "But to all who did receive him, who believed in his name, he gave the right to become children of God, who were born, not of blood nor of the will of the flesh nor of the will of man, but of God" (John 1:12–13 ESV). If you've accepted Jesus Christ, you are a child of God and a part of His amazing family for all eternity.

3-Minute Prayers for Families will help you come together as a family before God and share your faith with one another. It is our hope you will pray, study, learn, and grow in your love for God and for one another. Please take time to pray together and use the discussion questions as an opportunity to learn from one another.

THE EDITORS

Remember my words with your whole being. Write them down and tie them to your hands as a sign; tie them on your foreheads to remind you. Teach them well to your children, talking about them when you sit at home and walk along the road, when you lie down and when you get up.

DEUTERONOMY 11:18–19 NCV

Heavenly Father, as a family we want to learn Your ways. The Bible is a map for our lives that is filled with promises. We want to know Your Word and write it on our hearts. May we not only hear Your words, but take action. Let Your Word come alive in our family. Amen.

TALK ABOUT IT:

♥ What are some of the things God teaches us in His Word?

♥ When we choose to obey God's Word, what does that mean for our relationships with God and our family?

Words Can Hurt or Heal

*Let the words of my mouth and the meditation of
my heart be acceptable in Your sight, O Lord,
my [firm, impenetrable] Rock and my Redeemer.*
PSALM 19:14 AMP

Lord, help me understand that the words I say and the
things I do can either hurt or heal someone's heart. I want
to say good things to others. I want to fill their hearts with
love. I want to help them know how much I love them and
how much You love them. Help me think and talk in a way
that pleases You, even when I am angry or hurt. Amen.

TALK ABOUT IT:

- ♥ How do you feel when someone says something not
  nice to you?
- ♥ How do you feel when you say something hurtful to
  someone else?

When I Say, "Sorry"

*Wash me thoroughly from my iniquity, and cleanse
me from my sin. For I acknowledge my transgressions,
and my sin is always before me.*
PSALM 51:2-3 NKJV

Heavenly Father, when I do things I shouldn't do, I know I
should say I am sorry, but sometimes I don't want to. I can
be selfish and mean and hurt other people, and hurt You.
Help me to think about what pleases You. When I confess
my sin, I open the door of my heart and invite You in to
clean me up. I want to have a heart that is quick to ask for
forgiveness and quick to forgive others. Amen.

TALK ABOUT IT:

- ♥ Why do you think is it hard to say you're sorry?
- ♥ How do you feel when someone tells you that they are
  sorry for hurting you?

No Longer Afraid

For God gave us a spirit not of fear
but of power and love and self-control.
2 TIMOTHY 1:7 ESV

Dear God, sometimes I am afraid at night when it is dark.
The Bible promises me that I don't have to be afraid. You
have given me courage and faith to trust that You will
take care of me and keep me safe in everything I do. In the
darkness, You are with me. You watch over me as I sleep
and are with me throughout my day. Thank You for always
being there, for loving me, and helping me to know that I
don't have to be afraid. Amen.

TALK ABOUT IT:

- ♥ What makes you feel afraid?
- ♥ How does it make you feel knowing that God is always
  with you?

The Choice to Obey

"For I have come down from heaven to do the
will of God who sent me, not to do my own will."
JOHN 6:38 NLT

Jesus, when You walked on the earth 2,000 years ago, You
were a person just like me. You loved God like I do, and
You wanted to please Him. Maybe You sometimes were
tempted to do things differently than the way God wanted
You to, but You chose to obey God, Your Father. Help me
to choose God's ways. Help me to do the things that please
Him, just as You did. Remind me that it is better to obey
when I am selfish or difficult and want to do things my own
way. Amen.

• • 💜 • •

TALK ABOUT IT:

- 💜 Do you ever feel like your way is better than God's way?
- 💜 Is it hard to trust that God's way will be better for you
  because you chose to obey?

Say Only What Is True

*"God is not man, that he should lie, or a son of man,
that he should change his mind. Has he said, and will he
not do it? Or has he spoken, and will he not fulfill it?"*
NUMBERS 23:19 ESV

Jesus, I know that lying is wrong. Sometimes I think telling
a lie will make someone feel better or will get me out of
trouble, but I am learning how a lie can hurt me and hurt
others. You never lie. Every promise You make, You keep.
Everything You say in the Bible is truth. Help me to always
choose the truth no matter how hard it might be. Thank
You for being the best example. Please show me how to be
a good example of truth to others. Amen.

TALK ABOUT IT:

♥ How can lies hurt you and hurt other people?

♥ How can we help each other always tell the truth?

It's Okay to Ask for Help

I will lift up my eyes to the hills—from whence
comes my help? My help comes from the LORD,
who made heaven and earth.
PSALM 121:1-2 NKJV

God, I want to do things on my own. It makes me feel good
to know that I can do things without help from anyone else,
but there are times I need help—from You, and from my
family. Sometimes when I do something without the help
of others, I can get hurt. I can also miss an opportunity to
learn and grow by not letting others help. Teach me when
I need to ask for help and then teach me to be thankful for
Your help and for help from others. Amen.

• • ♥ • •

TALK ABOUT IT:

♥ How does it make you feel when you ask for help?

♥ Do you think your family wants to help you?

*Do not gloat over me, my enemies!
For though I fall, I will rise again. Though I
sit in darkness, the LORD will be my light.*
MICAH 7:8 NLT

Jesus, sometimes I have bad days. It feels like no matter how many times I try, I mess up over and over. When things seem hard, help me to look to You. You give me what I need to try again and again and do better next time. No matter what others say, You will help me. I am Your child, and You created me to be successful. Thank You for loving me and giving me courage to try again. Amen.

• ○ ♥ ○ •

TALK ABOUT IT:

♥ Why is it sometimes difficult to try again after messing up?

♥ How does Jesus help you get back up and try again?

*"Out of them shall come songs of thanksgiving,
and the voices of those who celebrate. I will multiply them,
and they shall not be few; I will make them honored,
and they shall not be small."*
JEREMIAH 30:19 ESV

Jesus, every day can be a celebration for my family. You
have given us hope in new life and a promise that we can
spend the rest of our lives here and forever in heaven with
You. We want good things to happen for our family, and
we celebrate when we receive Your blessings. Help us to
celebrate when others are blessed and You bring goodness
to their lives as well. Amen.

TALK ABOUT IT:

- ♥ How can we share the blessings the Lord has given us?

- ♥ Sometimes when good things happen for others,
  instead of us, how do we handle disappointment?

15

For Love's Sake

"This is my command: Love each other as I have loved you.
The greatest love a person can show
is to die for his friends."
JOHN 15:12-13 NCV

Jesus, You have told us to love one another. Sometimes
that is really hard because we want things our own way.
You have shown us that love gives others the best place at
the table or the biggest slice of cake. When I give up what
I want, I show love to my family and friends. You showed
me love by dying on the cross and giving Your life so that
I could live again. Help me to show my family and friends
Your love in what I do and say each day. Amen.

• • ♥ • •

TALK ABOUT IT:

♥ What are some ways you can show love to your
family?

♥ Talk about a time when you showed Jesus' love to
someone else.

A Blessing for the Child

"God bless you and keep you, God smile on you and gift you,
God look you full in the face and make you prosper."
NUMBERS 6:24-26 MSG

Heavenly Father, thank You for the gift of my children.
Thank You for the joy they bring to me. They are created in
Your image and filled with Your love. You have given them
all that they need to become the individuals You created
them to be. May they continue to grow in Your wisdom.
Keep them safe. May they know You every day of their
lives and never step off the path You have set before them.
Amen.

• • ♥ • •

TALK ABOUT IT:

- ♥ Discuss special gifts God has given each child.
- ♥ Ask the children what gifts they see in themselves that
  God has given them.

Put on an Attitude of Praise

*I will give thanks to the L*ORD *with my whole heart;*
I will recount all of your wonderful deeds. I will be
glad and exult in you; I will sing praise
to your name, O Most High.
PSALM 9:1-2 ESV

Lord, thank You for the many blessings You have given our family. Thank You for loving us and giving us whatever we need. Remind us to count our blessings. When we get up in the morning, we thank You for another day with You as a family. We are grateful that You keep us healthy and strong. We praise You because we are Your children and You know what we need before we even ask. Amen.

· · ♥ · ·

TALK ABOUT IT:

- ♥ What are some things you are thankful to the Lord for?
- ♥ What helps you to remember to praise Him for His goodness and love in your life?

In the day when I cried out, You answered me,
and made me bold with strength in my soul.
PSALM 138:3 NKJV

Heavenly Father, there are days that are hard and situations I don't want to face. Some mornings I don't want to go to school or work. There are things I feel like I can't do. Sometimes there are people who are mean. You know my life and my heart. You are my strength and You give me everything I need to do the things that seem impossible. Show me how to have a good attitude, focus on one thing at a time, and trust that with You, I can do anything. Amen.

• • ♥ • •

TALK ABOUT IT:

- ♥ When did God help you do something you didn't think you could do?
- ♥ Is there something you want to pray about for God to help you with now?

Provision: God Takes Care of Us

And this same God who takes care of me will
supply all your needs from his glorious riches,
which have been given to us in Christ Jesus.
PHILIPPIANS 4:19 NLT

God, You promise to take care of us. When it is hard for
us to know the difference between what we want and what
we really need, You know exactly what we need. Give our
family wisdom to make the best decisions for our lives.
Point us in the direction You would have our family to go
in work, church, school, and how to spend our time and
money. Amen.

* * ♥ * *

TALK ABOUT IT:

♥ How has God taken care of our family in the past?

♥ When do you feel well taken care of?

Angels Watching Over Me

He has put his angels in charge of you
to watch over you wherever you go.
PSALM 91:11 NCV

Jesus, thank You for putting Your angels in charge of watching over me. I trust that You will take care of me and keep me safe. You will lead me in the way I should go and keep my path straight and clear. Help me to hear from You so that I am in the right place at the right time, every time. Give me wisdom, and guide me as I follow Your instruction in every decision throughout my day. Amen.

· · ♥ · ·

TALK ABOUT IT:

♥ Do you ever feel like you need to go a different route home than you normally do or that you should leave a little later than normal? Could that be God's influence protecting you?

Out with the Old, In with the New

Therefore be imitators of God,
as beloved children.
EPHESIANS 5:1 ESV

God, we all have habits—good and bad. As Your child,
I am created to look like You and follow Your example
of goodness. I want to create good habits in my life that
reflect Your goodness and love. Help me to see the habits
I have that are not good. When I do something that is not
like You, speak softly to my heart and remind me to choose
to do good, like You. Amen.

• • ♥ • •

TALK ABOUT IT:

- ♥ What are some good habits you have that remind you of God's goodness?
- ♥ What are some bad habits you need to ask God to help you stop doing?

The Importance of "God-Friends"

The righteous should choose his friends carefully,
for the way of the wicked leads them astray.
PROVERBS 12:26 NKJV

Lord, thank You for bringing people into our lives to
encourage us and help us grow in our relationship with
You. Give each of us a heart that knows who You want
and who You don't want having an influence in our lives.
Help us to be kind to everyone, but to know which people
You would have us to invite to become our best God-
friends. Amen.

TALK ABOUT IT:

- ♥ There are people that encourage us, and people we are
  supposed to encourage. Why is it important to know
  the difference?

- ♥ How can you know the difference?

Jesus Your Healer

Dear friend, I hope all is well with you and that you are as healthy in body as you are strong in spirit.
3 JOHN 1:2 NLT

Jesus, when someone in our family is sick, we thank You for providing healing. Teach us to put the right food and drink into our bodies so that we live in good health. When we become sick, show us how to take good care of ourselves and get better. Thank You for wisdom You give to doctors and nurses to help us know what to do when we need assistance. Amen.

TALK ABOUT IT:

- ♥ What are some practical things you know to do that will keep you healthy?

- ♥ When you don't feel well, who do you go to in your family for prayer? Why?

Fully Satisfied

[And it is, indeed, a source of immense profit, for] godliness
accompanied with contentment (that contentment
which is a sense of inward sufficiency)
is great and abundant gain.
1 TIMOTHY 6:6 AMP

Lord, everywhere we look people are always wanting more.
While there is nothing wrong with having nice things, help
us to realize that we can be content and thankful for what
we do have. I want to be fully satisfied with what You give
me because You have promised to give me exactly what I
need. We are grateful for all You have given us. Amen.

· · ♥ · ·

TALK ABOUT IT:

- ♥ What does it mean to be satisfied?
- ♥ How often do you tell God thank You?
- ♥ How often do you say thank you to your family?
- ♥ What are you most thankful for?

Grace at Work

*Grace and peace to you from God our Father
and the Lord Jesus Christ.*
ROMANS 1:7 NCV

Jesus, thank You for the plan of salvation. Thank You for inviting us to experience God's grace and peace as a part of Your family. We want to be a holy family—set apart and dedicated to live a life acceptable and pleasing to You. Give us strength and hope to live each day in the promise to become all that You desire us to be. Amen.

· · ♥ · ·

TALK ABOUT IT:

♥ What does it mean to live a life that pleases Jesus?

♥ What does God's grace and peace mean to you?

*As he was drawing near—already on the way down the
Mount of Olives—the whole multitude of his disciples
began to rejoice and praise God with a loud voice
for all the mighty works that they had seen.*
LUKE 19:37 ESV

Heavenly Father, You are the miracle maker. Thank You for
all the miracles You have done. You are at work in building
our faith as we study Your Word. You grow our family as
we become closer to one another and understand each
other. You provide for us and keep us safe and healthy
each day. Thank You for the miracles that happen each
day—even when we don't see them. Amen.

TALK ABOUT IT:

♥ What are some of the miracles God has done for you
and your family?

♥ What does it mean to expect a miracle?

27

Goodbye to Past Mistakes

"The thief's purpose is to steal and kill and destroy.
My purpose is to give them a rich and satisfying life."
JOHN 10:10 NLT

God, You forgive and forget. Forgetting is the hard part
sometimes for me. When I make mistakes and bring
them to You, You wash them away and never remember
them. You never bring up the past. You let it go. It's hard
for me to forget, and others even remind me of things
I've done wrong. Help me to say goodbye to the past and
begin again. Each day is a new start, and I don't have to
go backward, but can move forward because You have
forgiven me. Amen.

· · ♥ · ·

TALK ABOUT IT:

♥ Is there something you need to ask forgiveness
  for. . . from God or from another person?

♥ How can you say goodbye to past mistakes?

The Lord Is with Us

*"Blessed shall you be when you come in,
and blessed shall you be when you go out."*
DEUTERONOMY 28:6 NKJV

Lord, our family can't always be together. There are
times throughout our day when we have to face the world
without each other. Your Word says that we are blessed
when we come in and when we go out. Remind us, Lord,
that each time we leave our home to go out into the world
that we are blessed because You go with us. Whatever
happens throughout the day, we are never alone—You are
with us—always! Amen.

· · ♥ · ·

TALK ABOUT IT:

♥ Kids, do you ever wish Mom or Dad could go with you
when they can't?

♥ Mom or Dad, how does it make you feel knowing the
Lord goes with each child and is with them even when
you can't be?

What My Eyes See

If your right eye serves as a trap to ensnare you or is an occasion for you to stumble and sin, pluck it out and throw it away. It is better that you lose one of your members than that your whole body be cast into hell.
MATTHEW 5:29 AMP

Jesus, my eyes are the window to my heart. What I see goes into my heart and affects what I think, feel, and do. I will protect my heart by looking at things that please You. There are things on television and on the Internet that I know I should not see. Help me to stand up for what is right when others say it's okay to do what I know might hurt me. Amen.

· · 💜 · ·

TALK ABOUT IT:

- 💜 When have you watched something that made you feel bad?
- 💜 How can you ask for help when you feel tempted to look at something you shouldn't?

No More Delays

*Jesus said, "No procrastination. No backward looks.
You can't put God's kingdom off till
tomorrow. Seize the day."*
LUKE 9:62 MSG

Jesus, You know that I don't always do what I know I should do right away. It's easy to do what I want to do—play a game or eat a snack—instead of clean my room or do my homework. I want to obey my parents and do what is right, but sometimes I lose track of time. Forgive me for when I disobey and help me to do those things I know I need to do first. I know that when I am obedient it pleases my parents and You. Amen.

· · 💙 · ·

TALK ABOUT IT:

💙 What can help you remember to do the things you don't really like to do first?

💙 How is it helpful to save the fun things for last?

Quality Time Together

Dear friends, we should love each other, because love comes from God. Everyone who loves has become God's child and knows God.
1 JOHN 4:7 NCV

God, our lives are full and sometimes it feels like there is not enough time in the day. But the truth is that what we value most is what we give our time to. Help us to see our family members as important. The activities we do each day fill up our time, but when it comes to what's really important, knowing and loving each other is what matters most. Show us how to demonstrate love to one another with the time we spend together. Amen.

• • ♥ • •

TALK ABOUT IT:

- ♥ When you can spend time with a family member, what does that mean to you?
- ♥ What do you like to do most as a family?

Prayer Power

*Therefore, confess your sins to one another and pray for
one another, that you may be healed. The prayer of
a righteous person has great power as it is working.*
JAMES 5:16 ESV

Heavenly Father, I like talking to You. You are always there
when I want to talk. When I pray, I trust that You hear
me. When I talk to You about my day and the concerns I
have, You take me seriously. When I feel like I can't talk
to anyone else, I can share things with You and know that
You will work things out in a way that is best for me. Amen.

TALK ABOUT IT:

- ♥ What do you like most about being able to talk to God?
- ♥ Is there anything you don't think you can share with
  Him? Why or why not?

A Good Laugh

*Then our mouth was filled with laughter, and our tongue with singing. Then they said among the nations, "The L*ORD* has done great things for them."*
PSALM 126:2 NKJV

Lord, it is good to laugh. You fill my mouth with laughter and my heart with singing. Give me a good sense of humor and help me to share it with my friends and family. You made me in Your image and I want to be like You. You created me for happiness and joy. When the unexpected happens, instead of being shocked or afraid, let me enjoy the moment and respond with laughter. Fill me with Your laughter and let me bring happiness to others. Amen.

• • ♥ • •

TALK ABOUT IT:

- ♥ When were you surprised when something serious became funny?
- ♥ What makes you laugh?
- ♥ How do you make others laugh?

*For it was fitting for Him, for whom are all things and
by whom are all things, in bringing many sons to glory,
to make the captain of their salvation
perfect through sufferings.*
HEBREWS 2:10 NKJV

Heavenly Father, family is important to You, so family
should be important to me. Thank You for choosing my
family. Give me grace to find my place within my family.
Give me words to speak that show my family how much I
love them and help them understand how important they
are to me. Thank You for a place to belong. I belong to
them just like I belong to You. Amen.

· · 💜 · ·

TALK ABOUT IT:

- 💜 God gave you your family. What are some things you
  really like about your family?

- 💜 What are some things that you wish were different?
  Take time to pray about those things together.

"But someone who does not know, and then does something wrong, will be punished only lightly. When someone has been given much, much will be required in return; and when someone has been entrusted with much, even more will be required."
LUKE 12:48 NLT

God, as we grow each day as individuals and as a family, we learn and understand more about who we are. Just as Mom and Dad give us responsibility according to our age and abilities, You also give us more responsibility to know what is right and wrong. Help us to hear Your voice and do what You instruct us to do. Amen.

• • ♥ • •

TALK ABOUT IT:

- ♥ What new responsibilities have Mom and Dad given you lately? How did that make you feel?
- ♥ What new things do you understand about God and His love for you?

Seeing God

Now faith is the assurance (the confirmation, the title deed) of the things [we] hope for, being the proof of things [we] do not see and the conviction of their reality [faith perceiving as real fact what is not revealed to the senses].
HEBREWS 11:1 AMP

Father, we believe in You. We trust that You are with us always. Although we cannot see the air we breathe, we know it is there. Just as the wind blows the trees and we see the evidence as the trees move, we can see You at work in our lives. We see You through the blessings You give us and the protection You provide our family each day. Amen.

TALK ABOUT IT:
- ♥ How have you seen God at work in your life?
- ♥ How does He let you know He is there?

Do you see what this means—all these pioneers who blazed the way, all these veterans cheering us on? It means we'd better get on with it. Strip down, start running—and never quit!
HEBREWS 12:1 MSG

Jesus, I am constantly learning new things. I am tempted to give up when life gets hard, but I know that You will help me do whatever I need to do. Give me patience to practice what I need to learn. Help me to work hard toward my goal. When I want to quit, help me to see the finish line. Thank You for my family who encourages me and cheers me on. Whatever I face, I know I can do it because You are on my side. Amen.

· · 💗 · ·

TALK ABOUT IT:

- 💜 What things are hard for you?
- 💜 How can we work together as a family to help one another?

Everything Good!

"I say this because I know what I am planning for you,"
says the LORD. "I have good plans for you, not plans to
hurt you. I will give you hope and a good future."
JEREMIAH 29:11 NCV

I can't imagine my world without You, Lord. You put me
and my family on this earth for a reason. You have plans
for my life—not just after I grow up—but today and every
day. I can encourage others and point them to You. Thank
You for the hope of a great life and a great future, for me
and for my family. You are everything *good*! Amen.

TALK ABOUT IT:

♥ What do you want to see God do in your life and your
family?

♥ Where do you see God's goodness in other family
members?

Feeling Selfish

Let no one seek his own good,
but the good of his neighbor.
1 CORINTHIANS 10:24 ESV

God, You are good to us. You have promised to provide
everything we need. Everything we have comes from You.
Sometimes it is hard to share something that is special
or important to me. Speak to my heart and remind me to
be generous and thoughtful toward others, showing love,
especially to my own family members. When I am tempted
to be selfish, remind me that what I am holding close to my
heart was a gift from You. Amen.

TALK ABOUT IT:

♥ Why is it hard to share special things with others?

♥ What does it say about God's unselfishness when
He gave Jesus to us so that we could know Him
personally?

Your Promise in Me

Your eyes saw my unformed substance; in your book were written, every one of them, the days that were formed for me, when as yet there was none of them.
PSALM 139:16 ESV

Heavenly Father, You created me. You knew me before anyone else. You gave me the potential to become more than I can dream. Help my faith grow so I believe I can be all that You want me to be. I trust You to lead me where You want me to go and do what You want me to do. Give me wisdom and understanding to make good decisions—choices that will keep me pointed toward Your promise for my life. Amen.

• • 💜 • •

TALK ABOUT IT:

💜 What dreams do you have for your life?

💜 Where do you hope that God's promise will take you?

Responsible in Love

For we are each responsible for our own conduct.
GALATIANS 6:5 NLT

Lord, it's easy to blame someone else for how I act or feel.
The truth is I am responsible for how I respond to others.
When someone says something hurtful, I want to respond
in anger. When I make a mistake, it's easier to blame
someone else than to take responsibility. You created me
unique and special. There is no one like me. Help me to
show others Your love by my actions. Help me say I'm
sorry when I should. Today I will choose to be responsible
for what I do and say. Amen.

• • ♥ • •

TALK ABOUT IT:

- ♥ What are some things you want to be more
  responsible for?

- ♥ How can we, as a family, help each other be more
  responsible for our actions?

God Is Always There

Be strong, courageous, and firm; fear not nor be in terror
before them, for it is the Lord your God Who goes
with you; He will not fail you or forsake you.
DEUTERONOMY 31:6 AMP

God, sometimes I am afraid. But You have promised me
that I can be strong and courageous. I have nothing to fear
because You are with me always. You will never fail me, but
will always take good care of me. I have family and good
friends that reassure me when I worry about things. When
I feel afraid, I look up to heaven and remember You see me.
You know my heart and fill me with courage. I reach out
and take Your hand by faith. Amen.

• • ♥ • •

TALK ABOUT IT:

♥ How can you be strong in the middle of something
scary?

♥ How does it comfort you to know God is always there?

Waiting for God's Best

*GOD formed Man out of dirt from the ground
and blew into his nostrils the breath of life.
The Man came alive—a living soul!*
GENESIS 2:7 MSG

God, thank You for giving us life. You gave life to the
first man, Adam, and You've given us more. You gave us
Your Son, Jesus, so that we could know You personally.
You give us everything we need to live our lives. Help
us to understand that sometimes what we think we need
isn't always Your best plan. We want Your best, so show
us how to be patient and wait on Your perfect gifts.
Amen.

· · 💜 · ·

TALK ABOUT IT:

- 💜 Why do you think it is hard to wait on the things you
  want?
- 💜 What can you do to help you be more patient when
  you have to wait?

Building a Bridge with One Another

*Since we are justified (acquitted, declared righteous,
and given a right standing with God) through faith, let us
[grasp the fact that we] have [the peace of reconciliation
to hold and to enjoy] peace with God through our Lord
Jesus Christ (the Messiah, the Anointed One).*
ROMANS 5:1 AMP

God, sometimes feelings get hurt or we say things
we shouldn't say. You made a way for us to fix our
relationship with You through accepting Jesus as our
Lord and Savior. You built a bridge between us with the
cross so that we could forever be with You. Help us build
a bridge with Your love for one another in our family.
Help us to make things right today. Amen.

· ○ ♥ ○ ·

TALK ABOUT IT:

♥ Do you need to make something right with a family
member today?

♥ What can you do today to show that person love?

Second Chances

Behold, the Lord's hand is not shortened, that it cannot save; nor His ear heavy, that it cannot hear.
ISAIAH 59:1 NKJV

Thank You, Lord, for second chances. I love You and want to follow You, but sometimes my own way seems so right, or I am just stubborn and want to do it my way. When You ask me to obey You, I don't want to be like Jonah and run the opposite way. But, when I do, like Jonah, I ask You to forgive me. Thank You for the chance to obey You once again. When I mess things up, You rescue me and pull me out of the darkness into the light. Amen.

• • ♥ • •

TALK ABOUT IT:

- ♥ What did God ask Jonah to do? (See Jonah chapter 1.)
- ♥ How did Jonah disobey God?
- ♥ What did Jonah do to make it right?

Teachable Heart

Let the wise hear and increase in learning,
and the one who understands obtain guidance.
PROVERBS 1:5 ESV

Lord, each day is an opportunity for us to learn more about You, about our family, about the world around us, and about ourselves. Forgive us when we think we already know it all. The way we see life is different depending on where we stand. Our house looks very different when we look at it from the front yard, than when we see it from the backyard. Even when we've seen our house a hundred times from each angle, there is always a chance to see something new. Give us teachable hearts, open to see this beautiful world and our own lives from Your perspective each day. Amen.

TALK ABOUT IT:

♥ How does it make you feel to learn something new?

♥ What kind of things do you want God or your parents to teach you?

When Shortcuts Aren't Worth It

For we cannot oppose the truth,
but must always stand for the truth.
2 CORINTHIANS 13:8 NLT

Lord, when I'm tempted to take shortcuts, please help me to know which ones aren't worth it. Cheating on a paper, taking credit for someone else's work, or even telling a white lie because I think it might make someone feel better is not worth it. I am Your child, and I must choose the truth. When the truth isn't always clear, speak to my heart and show me what is right. I want to always stand for the truth! Amen.

· · 💜 · ·

TALK ABOUT IT:

- 💜 When has the truth been hard to see?

- 💜 When were shortcuts not worth it?

- 💜 Talk about a time that you were glad you chose the truth over a shortcut.

New Places

You shall establish yourself in righteousness (rightness, in conformity with God's will and order): you shall be far from even the thought of oppression or destruction, for you shall not fear, and from terror, for it shall not come near you.
ISAIAH 54:14 AMP

Heavenly Father, sometimes change can be a little scary. I know that You are always with me. You are there to comfort me when I have to step into the unfamiliar. Please fill me with Your peace when I am nervous about change. Help me to trust that You are leading and guiding me and my family. You know the direction we are going and will make our way clear and as easy as possible. Amen.

• • ♥ • •

TALK ABOUT IT:

♥ What do you do when you feel uneasy about changes?

♥ How do you handle unfamiliar places?

49

Heaven Is Real

*Abraham was confidently looking forward to a city
with eternal foundations, a city designed
and built by God.*
HEBREWS 11:10 NLT

Jesus, I know heaven is real, and someday I will spend
all my days there with You. Thank You for salvation and
knowing that I belong to You. Thank You for giving me
a purpose to live all of my days here on earth. Help me
to share Your love with others every day. I pray they see
Your love in me so that they will want to know You, too.
Then, when You come to take us to heaven, we can all go
together and live with You forever. Amen.

• • ♥ • •

TALK ABOUT IT:

♥ What do you think heaven will be like?

♥ Why is it important to live for God each day on earth?

Celebrate the Little Things

You will teach me how to live a holy life. Being with you
will fill me with joy; at your right hand I will
find pleasure forever.
PSALM 16:11 NCV

God, even the littlest things matter to You. The Bible
says You know how many hairs I have on my head right
now. You counted the stars and gave them names. The
things that are important to me are also important to You.
That gives me courage to share every little piece of my
life with You. I can tell You anything I'm thinking about
and You will listen. And when I bring You the hardest
things, I know You will understand. I don't have to wait for
something gigantic in my life to celebrate. It's important to
celebrate the little things, too. Amen.

· · 🖤 · ·

TALK ABOUT IT:

🖤 What are some little things you can celebrate today?

🖤 What little things can you thank God for?

Cheering Others On

So speak encouraging words to one another.
Build up hope so you'll all be together in this, no one
left out, no one left behind. I know you're already
doing this; just keep on doing it.
1 THESSALONIANS 5:11 MSG

Lord, I want to be a cheerleader for others by encouraging them. Instead of pointing out what others do wrong, help me to see the good things they do. Help me to notice good in each person and to boldly tell them what an excellent job he or she is doing. Show me how to build their faith with my words of encouragement. Amen.

· · 💜 · ·

TALK ABOUT IT:

💜 What words do you like to hear others say when they are cheering you on?

💜 What can you do when others are feeling down?

Everything Good

For the L<small>ORD</small> God is our sun and our shield.
He gives us grace and glory. The L<small>ORD</small> will withhold
no good thing from those who do what is right.
P<small>SALM</small> 84:11 <small>NLT</small>

Heavenly Father, I am learning that You want the very best for me. Sometimes what I think is best isn't always Your best. I can't help but be disappointed when things turn out differently than I want them to. Help me to trust You. Your best is always better than mine. You have promised in Your Word that You would never withhold anything good from me. Amen.

. . 💜 . .

TALK ABOUT IT:

- 💜 How do you feel when Mom or Dad don't think something you want is good for you?

- 💜 What does it mean to trust God (or Mom or Dad) for what they believe is good for you?

Honest and Good

*Honesty guides good people; dishonesty
destroys treacherous people.*
PROVERBS 11:3 NLT

Jesus, You are always honest. You have never told a lie,
even when it was something other people didn't want to
hear. When I think that a lie will get me out of trouble,
remind me that lies destroy trust and hurt those I love.
Help me to speak the truth and respond honestly in all
I say. Help me to speak the truth with love—never in a
hurtful way. I want to be an honest person that others can
trust! Amen.

TALK ABOUT IT:

♥ Share a time a lie was hurtful to you or your family.

♥ Share a time you were thankful you told the truth.

The Lord Keeps Us

Be not afraid of sudden terror and panic, nor of the stormy blast or the storm and ruin of the wicked when it comes [for you will be guiltless], for the Lord shall be your confidence, firm and strong, and shall keep your foot from being caught [in a trap or some hidden danger].
PROVERBS 3:25-26 AMP

Lord, I pray for my family. Thank You for keeping us safe. Sometimes the news we hear is not good, but sad and scary. You are our hope. No matter what report we hear on the news, Your report is good. We hear Your voice and follow. We can trust You to keep us, to show us the way to go, and bring us back home without fear. Amen.

TALK ABOUT IT:

♥ Tell your family about a time you believe the Lord kept you safe.

55

God, My Friend

And the Scripture was fulfilled which says, "Abraham believed God, and it was accounted to him for righteousness." And he was called the friend of God.
JAMES 2:23 NKJV

God, You are my friend. No matter where I am, You are with me. I can talk to You anytime, and I know You are listening. I can tell You all my hopes and dreams. When I am down I can tell You about the things that make me feel sad. Help me to listen to You and hear Your voice. Speak to my heart and tell me the things I need to know so that I may be the person You want me to be. Amen.

· • ♥ • ·

TALK ABOUT IT:

♥ What kind of things do you share with God?

♥ What is the best thing about your friendship with God?

Do not lie to one another, seeing that you have put off
the old self with its practices and have put on the new
self, which is being renewed in knowledge
after the image of its creator.
COLOSSIANS 3:9-10 ESV

Heavenly Father, some kids look like their moms or dads.
They have a family resemblance. I want to act and look
like You. When others see me, I want them to think of Your
love, mercy, grace, and goodness. When I make choices,
I pray that they are good and right. Let my actions and
decisions be more and more like You each day. Amen.

· · 🖤 · ·

TALK ABOUT IT:

🖤 Go around the room and have each family member
   share something they see in another person that
   reminds them of God.

Your kindness will reward you,
but your cruelty will destroy you.
PROVERBS 11:17 NLT

Lord, You want me to show kindness to others. Give me a more loving heart. When I look at other people, let me see them as You see them. Even when people are unkind or mean, help me to open my heart and speak kind words to them. I pray that through my kindness, they may see You in all I do. Amen.

TALK ABOUT IT:

- ♥ How do you feel when people are unkind to you? What is your first response?

- ♥ What can you do to help you remember to respond with kindness to others?

*To those who are pure, all things are pure, but to those
who are full of sin and do not believe, nothing is pure.
Both their minds and their consciences
have been ruined.*
TITUS 1:15 NCV

Jesus, You have saved me, healed me, and given me hope
and a future. My heart is clean and pure. Help me to keep
the truth of Your words at the center of my heart. As I know
Your truth more and more, I am able to see life as good,
pure, and right. I pray that others see me as someone who
brings hope and encouragement to their life, too. Amen.

· · 💜 · ·

TALK ABOUT IT:

💜 How do you see life? What good do you see in the
world around you?

God Our Promise Keeper

*Remember his covenant forever—the commitment
he made to a thousand generations.*
1 CHRONICLES 16:15 NLT

God, You made a promise to Abraham that You have kept
every day since You made it. Because You keep every
promise, I can trust You to do all that You say You will
do. Your Word, the Bible, is true. Even though I may have
doubt sometimes, help me to believe. If You say it, You
will do it, and I will trust You to keep Your promises every
day. Amen.

TALK ABOUT IT:

- What did God promise Abraham? (See Genesis 12.)
- How does it make you feel to know God is a promise
keeper?

God Is on Our Side

*What then shall we say to [all] this? If God is for us,
who [can be] against us? [Who can be our foe,
if God is on our side?]*
ROMANS 8:31 AMP

God, when You picked Your team, You picked me. Thank
You for choosing me and giving me an opportunity to
become Your child by accepting Your gift of salvation.
You will stand up for me, and when people choose to come
against me, they come against You. No matter what comes
my way, I know we're in it together. Amen.

TALK ABOUT IT:

- ♥ What does it mean to be righteous?
- ♥ Why is it important to have God on your side?

Jesus Wants You Well

"I urge you to pray for absolutely everything, ranging from small to large. Include everything as you embrace this God-life, and you'll get God's everything."

MARK 11:24 MSG

Jesus, You are my healer. You took every sickness and disease to the cross and defeated them all so that I could live my life free. As I do my part taking care of my body, eating things that are good for me and exercising, I trust that You will keep my body in good health. When I do need to go to the doctor, give my doctor wisdom for what is best for me. Amen.

· · 💙 · ·

TALK ABOUT IT:

- 💜 What happens when you eat things that are not good for you?
- 💜 Does your body give you signs that it needs you to stop and take care of yourself? What kind of signs?

Make Us Disciples

*You have not chosen Me, but I have chosen you and
I have appointed you [I have planted you], that you might
go and bear fruit and keep on bearing, and that your fruit
may be lasting [that it may remain, abide], so that
whatever you ask the Father in My Name [as presenting
all that I AM], He may give it to you.*
JOHN 15:16 AMP

Lord, You have chosen me to be Your disciple, to learn
from You and follow You all of my days. Teach me Your
ways. As I open the Bible, help me to hear Your voice and
discover truths about You and the life You want me to live.
Give me strength to do things Your way instead of my own
way. Amen.

TALK ABOUT IT:

- How does God speak to you?
- How does obeying your parents help you learn to
  follow the Lord?

63

My Good Shepherd

"My sheep listen to my voice; I know them, and they follow me. I give them eternal life, and they will never die, and no one can steal them out of my hand."
JOHN 10:27-28 NCV

Jesus, thank You for Your love and guidance. You are my Good Shepherd. You care for me as a loving and kind shepherd cares for His sheep. I listen for Your voice to lead me and guide me. You keep me safe from any harm as I go where You lead me. You watch me and always know where I am. Thank You that when I lag behind, You gently bring me back to the place of safety. Amen.

· · ♥ · ·

TALK ABOUT IT:

♥ When has the Lord helped you to stay on the path He has for you?

Great Expectations

"Master, we have toiled all night and caught nothing;
nevertheless at Your word I will let down the net."
And when they had done this, they caught a great
number of fish, and their net was breaking.
LUKE 5:5–6 NKJV

Jesus, thank You for the opportunity to know You more.
Thank You for saving me and giving me hope and a future.
I have big dreams that I can reach. Because of You, I don't
have to settle for average, but instead can expect great
things in my life. Amen.

TALK ABOUT IT:

- ♥ What good things has Jesus done for you and in you
  this week?

- ♥ Talk to God and your family about the things you want
  to see God do in your life.

Count on God's Love

"For the mountains may move and the hills disappear,
but even then my faithful love for you will remain.
My covenant of blessing will never be broken,"
says the Lord, who has mercy on you.
ISAIAH 54:10 NLT

God, thank You for loving us. We love You and choose to obey You. We are thankful that Your love is unconditional. There is nothing we can do that would cause You to take away Your love from us—no matter how many mistakes we make, no matter how many times we fail. You always are there to comfort us and forgive us. When we call for help, You always rescue us. Your love never ends. Amen.

· · ♥ · ·

TALK ABOUT IT:

♥ In what ways do you count on God's love?

♥ What does "unconditional love" mean?

*In peace I will both lie down and sleep, for You, Lord,
alone make me dwell in safety and confident trust.*
PSALM 4:8 AMP

Lord, when I go to bed at night, I will not be afraid. I
am safe and my family is safe. No matter what happens
through the night, You will take care of me and those I
love. Fill my heart and mind with Your peace. Give me
sweet dreams from heaven as I put my mind on You this
night. I trust You to keep each one of us as we sleep. Amen.

· · ♥ · ·

TALK ABOUT IT:

- ♥ Does the Lord sleep?

- ♥ Since He doesn't sleep, He is awake and watching over
  you as you rest. How does that make you feel?

Repay Bad with Good

Do not repay evil for evil or reviling for reviling,
but on the contrary, bless, for to this you were called,
that you may obtain a blessing.
1 PETER 3:9 ESV

Heavenly Father, some people are okay with tearing
others down to try to make themselves look good or
paying someone back for a wrong done to them. That is
not Your way. It is never right to insult or hurt another
person. Instead, the Bible encourages us to look to You,
forgive them, and pray for them. When I am hurt and want
revenge, help me to choose Your way and repay their bad
with Your good. Amen.

TALK ABOUT IT:

- ♥ When someone hurt you, how did you respond to
  them?
- ♥ Why do you think God wants you to repay them with
  good?

A Tender Heart

Get rid of all bitterness, rage, anger, harsh words,
and slander, as well as all types of evil behavior.
Instead, be kind to each other, tenderhearted, forgiving
one another, just as God through Christ has forgiven you.
EPHESIANS 4:31-32 NLT

Lord, sometimes it's hard for us all to get along. Even when we don't mean it, we say things we shouldn't and do things we know are unlike You. Give each of us a tender heart toward one another. Help us to think about our words or actions before we do or say them. We want to have a strong family that loves, trusts, and respects one another. Amen.

• • ♥ • •

TALK ABOUT IT:

♥ What does it mean to trust or respect one another?

♥ What has someone in your family done or said lately that made you feel loved?

69

Choices

*"You did not choose me; I chose you. And I gave you
this work: to go and produce fruit, fruit that will last.
Then the Father will give you anything
you ask for in my name."*
JOHN 15:16 NCV

Thank You, Jesus, for choosing to love me. You gave Your
life so I would have a choice—a choice to ask You into my
heart so I could live with You forever. Today, I choose You.
I want to live each day with You, knowing we will always be
together. Amen.

• • 💜 • •

TALK ABOUT IT:

- 💜 Think about how much Jesus loved you—so much that
  He gave His life so you could live. Does that make you
  love Him more?
- 💜 How can you show Jesus that you choose Him today?

Peace Instead of Perfection

*Love never gives up. Love cares more for others than
for self. Love doesn't want what it doesn't have.
Love doesn't strut, doesn't have a swelled head.*
1 Corinthians 13:4 MSG

God, Your love is patient, willing to wait, extending
grace. Sometimes my family gets on my nerves, hurts my
feelings, and irritates me. I want things to be perfect, but
it's not going to be that way. Fill me with Your love and
help me to see my family like You do—help me love them
with a heart like Yours. Show me how to look for peace
instead of perfection. Amen.

• • ♥ • •

TALK ABOUT IT:

- ♥ What does it mean when family members "push your
  buttons"?

- ♥ What choices can you make to look for peace in
  situations with your family?

A Christ-Like Attitude

I may give away everything I have, and I may even
give my body as an offering to be burned.
But I gain nothing if I do not have love.
1 CORINTHIANS 13:3 NCV

Heavenly Father, You can look into my heart and see whether my attitude is right or wrong. I can pretend like everything is good, when I actually have a bad attitude about something. Clean out my heart where I try to hide the ugly things that I think or feel. Help me to let them go, so that my heart is free to express and accept Your love. Thank You for loving me no matter what. Amen.

• • 💜 • •

TALK ABOUT IT:

💜 As a family, pray for each person to have a Christ-like attitude.

Thank You for My Family

*God sets the solitary in families; He brings out
those who are bound into prosperity; but the
rebellious dwell in a dry land.*
PSALM 68:6 NKJV

God, thank You for my family. They know me and
love me. I want to bring joy to them. Give me words of
encouragement to share with them. Help me to speak with
love. Teach me to be a good listener so that I may learn
how I can help them. Thank You for wisdom to understand
how I fit in my family and where my talents are best used
for Your kingdom and for my family. Amen.

TALK ABOUT IT:

- ♥ What makes you a good listener?

- ♥ How do you feel when you know someone has heard
  what you had to say?

Prayers for Dad and Mom

He must manage his own family well,
having children who respect and obey him.
1 TIMOTHY 3:4 NLT

God, thank You for my dad and mom. Thank You for giving me parents who love You and want to do what is good and right. Give me a heart that is open to hear You through their teachings. Please speak to them and through them as they train me in the way You want me to go. Help me to listen to them and trust them in the decisions for our family. Amen.

TALK ABOUT IT:

- ♥ Tell your parents one thing you like about them.
- ♥ Share with your parents something you would like to do together.

I Am God's Favorite, Too!

*Glory and honor and peace for everyone who does
good, the Jew first and also the Greek.
For God shows no partiality.*
ROMANS 2:10-11 ESV

Heavenly Father, it's hard when I feel left out. But the Bible
says that You love each of us the most and best. Thank You
that I can always feel like I am Your favorite child because
You show unconditional love. I am loved by You and by my
parents. Make that truth grow strong in my heart. Amen.

TALK ABOUT IT:

- ♥ Talk about a time that you felt special to your parents
  or another family member.

- ♥ There are many ways to show people you care—giving
  affection, saying words of praise and appreciation,
  spending time together. How do you know someone
  cares about you?

Shut the Lion's Mouth

"My God sent his angel, who closed the mouths of the lions so that they would not hurt me. I've been found innocent before God and also before you, O king. I've done nothing to harm you."

DANIEL 6:22 MSG

God, there are some not-so-nice people in this world. They say and do mean things. When I face people like this, help me to do what is right. Daniel was wrongfully accused and put into a den of hungry lions, but You shut the lions' mouths and kept him safe. I ask You to shut the mouths of those who speak mean and hurtful things to me, just as You shut the lions' mouths. Amen.

· · 🖤 · ·

TALK ABOUT IT:

- 🖤 Talk to your family about bullies. Are you having a tough time with someone?
- 🖤 Take time to pray for the bully so that they may come to know the love of God.

Ask for Help

Later, when Moses' arms became tired, the men put a large rock under him, and he sat on it. Then Aaron and Hur held up Moses' hands—Aaron on one side and Hur on the other. They kept his hands steady until the sun went down. So Joshua defeated the Amalekites in this battle.
EXODUS 17:12-13 NCV

Lord, sometimes I think I can do something by myself and then later realize I need help. Help me not to be stubborn or become angry when I can't do things on my own, but instead give me courage to ask for help. Thank You for family that are willing to help me when I need them. Amen.

· · ♥ · ·

TALK ABOUT IT:

♥ When did you need help, but didn't ask for it?

♥ Tell about times you were glad you asked for help.

Helping Others

Bear (endure, carry) one another's burdens and troublesome moral faults, and in this way fulfill and observe perfectly the law of Christ (the Messiah) and complete what is lacking [in your obedience to it].
GALATIANS 6:2 AMP

Jesus, You are always ready to help. Forgive me for being selfish by doing my own thing instead of helping others. When people ask for help, remind me that this is a good chance to show that I love them. Give me a heart to help! Amen.

• • ♥ • •

TALK ABOUT IT:

- ♥ How do you help around the house?
- ♥ What is your favorite chore? Your least favorite?

Storing Good Treasure

"For out of the abundance of the heart the mouth speaks. A good man out of the good treasure of his heart brings forth good things, and an evil man out of the evil treasure brings forth evil things."

MATTHEW 12:34-35 NKJV

God, You created my heart to be a treasure chest. Whatever feelings I have—good or bad—store up and eventually overflow out of my mouth. When I am angry, upset, and unforgiving, those feelings eventually boil over and I say something hurtful. Focus my heart's treasure chest on You, and give me wisdom to express my emotions in a good and godly way. Amen.

· · 💜 · ·

TALK ABOUT IT:

- 💜 When you are hurt or angry, what can you do to help those thoughts and feelings not boil over?

- 💜 What is a good way to resolve problems without hurtful words?

Not of This World

*Don't copy the behavior and customs of this world,
but let God transform you into a new person by changing
the way you think. Then you will learn to know God's
will for you, which is good and pleasing and perfect.*
ROMANS 12:2 NLT

Jesus, You opened the door to new life and a new way of living. When the world tells me that something is fun, but it goes against Your Word, help me to remember that I am choosing life and truth! I belong to You, so my life looks and feels different from those who don't know You. Thank You for giving me a better life. Amen.

· · ♥ · ·

TALK ABOUT IT:

- ♥ What are some things that make you different from those who don't know the Lord?
- ♥ How can your choices point others to Him?

Saying "I'm Sorry"

Confess your sins to one another and pray for one another,
that you may be healed. The prayer of a righteous
person has great power as it is working.
JAMES 5:16 ESV

Heavenly Father, it's not easy to admit when I'm wrong. But I can always come to You and say I'm sorry, and You will wipe away the wrong as if it never happened. It is harder to take things back when I hurt others. Help me to ask for forgiveness and really mean it. Amen.

TALK ABOUT IT:

♥ How does your heart feel when you say you're sorry, but you really don't mean it?

♥ What does it mean to know that your heavenly Father forgives you? And when others forgive you?

Wanting What God Wants

*"The person who obeys my heavenly Father's will
is my brother and sister and mother."*
MATTHEW 12:50 MSG

God, I love You and I know You love me. You want the best
for me just like my family does. When what I want and
what You want are not the same, speak to my heart and
show me Your truth. Help me to trust Your way instead of
my own. Amen.

TALK ABOUT IT:

- ♥ How do you know what is God's way of doing
  something?
- ♥ When you study the Bible, what are some of the things
  you have learned about God and His ways?

The Whole World in His Hands

*In the beginning God (prepared, formed, fashioned, and)
created the heavens and the earth.*
GENESIS 1:1 AMP

God, You started it all—You created the heavens and the
earth. You hold the whole wide world and everything in it
in Your hands. You put the planets in motion and the stars
in the sky. You tell the water in the ocean just how far it can
come up on the sand. You take care of everything in and
on the earth—even me. I don't have to worry because I trust
You to take care of every detail of my life. Amen.

TALK ABOUT IT:

♥ Are you worried about something today?

♥ Share it with your family and then pray together,
  giving that worry to God to work it out for you in His
  time.

"Accept the God of your father. Serve him completely and willingly, because the LORD knows what is in everyone's mind. He understands everything you think. If you go to him for help, you will get an answer."
1 CHRONICLES 28:9 NCV

God, I want to know You better. You are my God and my friend. You know my heart—what I think and do and why I do it. Give me a desire to study the Bible so that I can know You more and understand Your plans and purposes for my life. I want to know You more! Amen.

TALK ABOUT IT:

♥ What kinds of things do you tell God when you pray?

♥ What questions do you have for God?

Devotion to God

" 'You shall love the LORD your God with all your heart,
with all your soul, with all your strength, and with
all your mind,' and 'your neighbor as yourself.' "
LUKE 10:27 NKJV

Lord, I love You! Just as You gave Your life for me, I give
my life back to You. Teach me how everything I say and
do should reflect You and demonstrate the love I have
for You to others. When people see me, I want them to
think of You. Pour Your love out on me. Fill me up to
overflowing so that I spill out with Your love and share it
with others. Amen.

• • 💜 • •

TALK ABOUT IT:

- 💜 How can people see the Lord when they see you?
- 💜 How do you show the Lord you love Him?
- 💜 What does it look like when you see God in others?

I Count on You

The LORD is my rock, my fortress, and my savior; my God is my rock, in whom I find protection. He is my shield, the power that saves me, and my place of safety.
PSALM 18:2 NLT

God, when I need You, You are there. When I am afraid, I can ask for Your peace. You fill me with strength. Your presence comforts me. I can always count on You, just like I count on my family to be there for me. But even when they can't be with me, You are there for me. I want to be there for You, God. When You ask me to do something, remind me of Your faithfulness. Amen.

TALK ABOUT IT:

- ♥ When did you call on God last? How did He help you?
- ♥ What is something that God has asked you to do?

Giving Credit to God

"Return to your home, and declare how much God has done for you." And he went away, proclaiming throughout the whole city how much Jesus had done for him.
LUKE 8:39 ESV

God, everything that happens in my life that is good comes from You. Thank You for blessing my family. When good things happen, remind us that we're not the ones who made something happen, but it is Your mercy and goodness that brings blessings to us. You should get the credit! We give You honor by telling others of Your provision and love to each of us in our family. Thank You, God! Amen.

· · 🤍 · ·

TALK ABOUT IT:

- 🤍 When was the last time you gave God credit for doing something good in your life?
- 🤍 Share something with the family that God has done for you.

With God

*God can do anything, you know—far more than you could
ever imagine or guess or request in your wildest dreams!
He does it not by pushing us around but by working
within us, his Spirit deeply and gently within us.*
EPHESIANS 3:20 MSG

God, sometimes I get ahead of You—like when we go
shopping and I get ahead of my parents. When I am out in
front, You are no longer leading me. I don't want to be on
my own—I need Your leadership. Teach me to watch You,
even when I'm excited about where You're taking me in
life. Amen.

· · ♥ · ·

TALK ABOUT IT:

- ♥ Have you ever gotten lost in a store because you
  strayed away from your parents? How did that feel?

- ♥ How can you let God lead you? How does God lead
  your family?

It's Okay to Be Sad

The Lord is close to those who are of a broken heart and saves such as are crushed with sorrow for sin and are humbly and thoroughly penitent.
PSALM 34:18 AMP

Lord, we live in a world that brings bad news. There are things that make me sad. Thank You that I can talk to You and to my family about those things. It's okay to feel down sometimes. You understand how I feel. But that sadness doesn't have to last forever. You promise to give me joy and new hope. Amen.

TALK ABOUT IT:

- ♥ What are some things you feel sad about?
- ♥ How does it make you feel to know you can talk to the Lord and to your family about those things?

"If you keep quiet at this time, someone else will help and save the Jewish people, but you and your father's family will all die. And who knows, you may have been chosen queen for just such a time as this."
ESTHER 4:14 NCV

Heavenly Father, You are at work in our lives even when we can't see it. You know every single detail of my life. You know where I should be and when I should be there. Help me to be more aware of Your presence in my day. Remind me that You are always there. Amen.

· · ♥ · ·

TALK ABOUT IT:

♥ Throughout the book of Esther, God's name is not mentioned, but He makes Himself known. Discuss some times when God was at work in your life and family, even when you couldn't see Him.

When Bad Things Happen

*My brethren, count it all joy when you fall into various
trials, knowing that the testing of your
faith produces patience.*
JAMES 1:2-3 NKJV

Jesus, sometimes bad things happen and we don't
understand why. That's when I must put my hope and trust
in You. Just like I can't see what is in front of me in the
dark, I can't see what is on the other side of this hard time.
But You know what is on the other side. You lead me and
guide me through the darkness and bring me back into the
light. I choose to trust You. Amen.

TALK ABOUT IT:

- ♥ How is trusting God sometimes like walking through
  a dark room?

- ♥ How do you feel when the lights come back on?

To Know God's Word

For the word of God is alive and powerful. It is sharper
than the sharpest two-edged sword, cutting between soul
and spirit, between joint and marrow. It exposes
our innermost thoughts and desires.
HEBREWS 4:12 NLT

God, the Bible is filled with words written for me. Each
time I open it, I can grow in my faith and come to
understand more about You. When I am tempted to read it
like a book, instead of the living Word of God, remind me
to stop and listen. I open my heart and wait to hear what
You are saying to me. Amen.

TALK ABOUT IT:

- ♥ What do you like most about reading the Bible?
- ♥ How do you feel when you read it?
- ♥ How does God speak to you?

Doing Something Hard

And he said, "My presence will go with you,
and I will give you rest."
EXODUS 33:14 ESV

Jesus, there are days when I have to do things that I don't enjoy. It might be a chore I don't like, or I have to talk to someone that I don't want to talk to. I can put it off, but eventually I am going to have to face that thing and do it. Thank You for Your promise to go with me, to be with me, and to help me to do those difficult things. Help me to do them with the right attitude. Amen.

TALK ABOUT IT:

- ♥ Is there something you need to do that you've been putting off? What is it?

- ♥ Would it help you if a family member helped you? Ask them to help.

On Purpose

*Long before we first heard of Christ and got our hopes
up, he had his eye on us, had designs on
us for glorious living.*
EPHESIANS 1:12 MSG

Lord, Your plans for me are good! I was born with a
purpose and You put that dream in my heart from the
beginning of time. You placed me with the perfect family
that would help me develop and become all that You
want me to be. I am determined, no matter what stands in
my way, to become all that You see in me. Thank You for
giving me hope and a purpose. Amen.

· · ♥ · ·

TALK ABOUT IT:

- ♥ What do you like to do?
- ♥ Parents: Share how a childhood dream became a part
  of God's plan in your life.

The Whole House

If it seems evil to you to serve the Lord, choose for yourselves this day whom you will serve, whether the gods which your fathers served on the other side of the River, or the gods of the Amorites, in whose land you dwell; but as for me and my house, we will serve the Lord.
JOSHUA 24:15 AMP

Lord, we give You our lives and dedicate our entire household to know You more each day. May we grow closer to one another as we pursue a deeper relationship with You. Let our hearts be kind and generous toward others—especially within our own family. Amen.

• • ♥ • •

TALK ABOUT IT:

- ♥ What does it look like to serve the Lord as a family each day?

- ♥ What things do you do together for Him and for one another?

95

Blessed for Generations

But the LORD's love for those who respect him continues forever and ever, and his goodness continues to their grandchildren and to those who keep his agreement and who remember to obey his orders.
PSALM 103:17–18 NCV

Heavenly Father, thank You for my spiritual heritage that I can pass on to my children and children's children. Bless those who have been great examples to me. Thank You for the opportunity to lead and guide others in faith as we all work together to live our lives pleasing to You. Give me words of encouragement that bring hope to my family. Amen.

· · ♥ · ·

TALK ABOUT IT:

- ♥ What do you enjoy most about sharing Christ with others?
- ♥ How do you encourage others to know Christ?
- ♥ How do others help you grow in Him?

To Rest in Him

You will keep him in perfect peace, whose mind
is stayed on You, because he trusts in You.
ISAIAH 26:3 NKJV

Heavenly Father, there are days when we overthink
things—lay awake trying to figure out how to resolve
issues in our lives. But You are never too busy for even the
smallest things that weigh heavy on our hearts. Instead of
thinking about the day and what we might have done right
or wrong, help us to turn our thoughts to You. We think of
how much You love us, how You are always there for us,
and how You work all things together for our good. You are
our peace. Amen.

TALK ABOUT IT:

♥ What can you do to keep your thoughts on God and
   His goodness, instead of the worries of the day?

Josiah was eight years old when he became king, and he reigned in Jerusalem thirty-one years. He did what was pleasing in the LORD's sight and followed the example of his ancestor David. He did not turn away from doing what was right.
2 CHRONICLES 34:1-2 NLT

Lord, when we are kids, there are many things in life that we have to wait to do until we grow up, but serving You is not one of them. No matter how old or young we are, You can use us. Teach me honor You in all I do—starting now. Give me wisdom and help me to make the right choices in life. Amen.

TALK ABOUT IT:

♥ What can you do today that points others to God?

Precious in His Sight

"See that you do not despise one of these little ones.
For I tell you that in heaven their angels always see
the face of my Father who is in heaven."
MATTHEW 18:10 ESV

Jesus, living in an adult world can be very hard for little
ones. You see children—and all the potential You have put
within each one. Help us to value one another no matter
how young or old we are. You put each of us on the earth
to contribute to Your kingdom. You have put Your Word
in our hearts to speak life to one another and to bless one
another with all that is good through You. Amen.

・ ・ ♥ ・ ・

TALK ABOUT IT:

- ♥ Do you sometimes feel overlooked by others?
- ♥ How does it make you feel to know that Jesus sees you
  and knows you?

99

Room to Grow

Jesus matured, growing up in both body and spirit,
blessed by both God and people.
LUKE 2:52 MSG

Heavenly Father, everything You created is made to grow—
plants, trees, animals, and me! You give me food for my
body to grow, but You've given me what I need to grow
spiritually as well. Give me a hunger for Your presence, a
desire for prayer, and a need for Your wisdom found in the
Bible. Amen.

TALK ABOUT IT:

- ♥ What things can you do to grow spiritually?
- ♥ What goals can you set as a family to help one another
  grow spiritually?

Always Willing to Learn

In the same way, younger people should be willing to be under older people. And all of you should be very humble with each other. "God is against the proud, but he gives grace to the humble."
1 PETER 5:5 NCV

God, I want to have a teachable heart. Help me to realize that I can learn from anyone You bring into my life. Because we all have different experiences and different stories, we have much to give to one another. Never let me think I cannot listen to those younger than me or that someone older than me doesn't understand my generation. You may be speaking to me through them! Amen.

• • 🧡 • •

TALK ABOUT IT:

- 🧡 What is something you have learned by listening to someone younger than you?

- 🧡 What have you discovered as someone older than you shared their stories with you?

"All your children shall be taught by the LORD,
and great shall be the peace of your children."
ISAIAH 54:13 ESV

Lord, as I raise my children in Your ways, thank You
for instructing me with Your wisdom. Give me words
of encouragement to speak into their lives. Help me to
discipline them with love. Open their hearts to receive
Your instruction and truth. Let my words be Your words,
and may they be easily understood. Thank You for the
promise that they can know Your peace! Amen.

TALK ABOUT IT:

♥ What does it mean to be taught in the ways of the
Lord?

♥ How do your parents lead and guide you to know the
Lord?

Complete in Christ

Entering into this fullness is not something you figure out or achieve. It's not a matter of being circumcised or keeping a long list of laws. No, you're already in—insiders—not through some secretive initiation rite but rather through what Christ has already gone through for you, destroying the power of sin.
COLOSSIANS 2:11 MSG

Jesus, You are life. You are everything I need—You have all the answers to the questions I face in life. You are with me—You live in my heart. Sometimes I go back to thinking the old ways are okay, but then You remind me that I don't have to settle for the old. You have given me a new life and a new direction. Amen.

• • ♥ • •

TALK ABOUT IT:

♥ How is your life different now because Christ lives in you?

Faithful Obedience

Therefore, my dear ones, as you have always obeyed [my suggestions], so now, not only [with the enthusiasm you would show] in my presence but much more because I am absent, work out (cultivate, carry out to the goal, and fully complete) your own salvation with reverence and awe and trembling (self-distrust, with serious caution, tenderness of conscience, watchfulness against temptation, timidly shrinking from whatever might offend God and discredit the name of Christ).
PHILIPPIANS 2:12 AMP

Lord, there are times I don't want to obey—my parents or You. When I don't feel like obeying, please work in my heart. I want to do what pleases my parents, because pleasing them also pleases You. As I learn to obey them and follow their examples, I also learn to obey You. Amen.

• • ♥ • •

TALK ABOUT IT:

♥ How have you learned to follow the Lord because of your parents' example?

Come Closer to God

Do you know where your fights and arguments come from?
They come from the selfish desires that war within you....
Come near to God, and God will come near to you.
JAMES 4:1, 8 NCV

Heavenly Father, instead of fighting to get what I want, show me how to be thankful for the gifts You give me. As I move closer to You, I will want what You want. Help me to let go of selfishness as I trust You to give me and my family the things we really need. Amen.

TALK ABOUT IT:

- ♥ What does it feel like to be selfish?
- ♥ How does your attitude and actions change when you want to please God?

*Now the fruit of righteousness is sown in peace
by those who make peace.*
JAMES 3:18 NKJV

God, forgive me when I say mean, hurtful things to others.
My words show what is truly in my heart. Ugly words show
everyone else that my heart is not filled with Your presence
and peace. When I speak words displeasing to You, it tells
me that I need a change from the inside out. Clean my
heart today, and give me self-control so that my words
bring peace to those I love. Amen.

TALK ABOUT IT:

- ♥ Give some examples of words that hurt versus words
  that help.
- ♥ Say something encouraging to each family member
  today.

"Then if my people who are called by my name will humble themselves and pray and seek my face and turn from their wicked ways, I will hear from heaven and will forgive their sins and restore their land."

2 CHRONICLES 7:14 NLT

Thank You, God, for hearing my prayers. Help me to understand that prayer isn't just me talking to You, but is a conversation between the two of us. Help me not to be in a hurry when I pray, but instead give me patience to listen quietly to Your voice. Then give me courage to obey what You instruct me to do. Amen.

• • ♥ • •

TALK ABOUT IT:

- ♥ What are some ways that God speaks to you?
- ♥ What do you imagine God's voice sounds like?

107

Holy Spirit Is My Helper

Likewise the Spirit helps us in our weakness. For we do not know what to pray for as we ought, but the Spirit himself intercedes for us with groanings too deep for words.
ROMANS 8:26 ESV

Heavenly Father, thank You for sending the Holy Spirit to help us. There are times when we don't know what to say or how to pray, but the Holy Spirit will give us the words to pray. When we face challenges—in our health, finances, relationships, or any area of life—we can trust that You are at work in our lives bringing good. I pray the Holy Spirit will lead and guide us in all things, directing us to do what is good and right, according to Your plan! Amen.

• • 💜 • •

TALK ABOUT IT:

💜 Who do you talk to when you are unsure about something?

A Never-Ending Conversation

Be cheerful no matter what; pray all the time; thank God no matter what happens. This is the way God wants you who belong to Christ Jesus to live.
1 THESSALONIANS 5:16-18 MSG

God, You are with me always. I can talk to You any moment of my day. Whether it is a thought, a whisper, or a conversation—I know You are listening to what I have to say. Each time I talk to You, we can just start again wherever we left off. Thank You for knowing me and keeping me in all Your ways. Amen.

· · 💜 · ·

TALK ABOUT IT:

- 💜 Where do you think would be the strangest place to pray?
- 💜 When you are tired or irritated, what helps you to remember to praise God anyway?

Confident Prayer

Let us then fearlessly and confidently and boldly draw near to the throne of grace (the throne of God's unmerited favor to us sinners), that we may receive mercy [for our failures] and find grace to help in good time for every need [appropriate help and well-timed help, coming just when we need it].
HEBREWS 4:16 AMP

God, when I pray, I know You hear me. The things that matter to me, matter to You—even the smallest things. Thank You for allowing me to come to You any time. Your door is always open. You're never too busy to hear me. Help me not to be too busy or too distracted to listen. Amen.

· · ♥ · ·

TALK ABOUT IT:

♥ What kinds of things can distract you when you pray?

♥ How can you keep your mind on God when you pray?

God Sees Your Heart

*But the L*ORD *said to Samuel, "Don't look at how handsome
Eliab is or how tall he is, because I have not chosen him.
God does not see the same way people see. People look at
the outside of a person, but the L*ORD *looks at the heart."*
1 SAMUEL 16:7 NCV

Lord, sometimes I judge others by how they look, how they
dress, or how they act. They're different than me, and that
makes me uncomfortable. But You made every person in
Your image, and You love people who are like me and who
are very different from me. Teach me to see them as You
see them. Amen.

TALK ABOUT IT:

♥ Do you sometimes judge others wrongly?

God—Your Strength

Therefore I take pleasure in infirmities, in reproaches,
in needs, in persecutions, in distresses, for Christ's sake.
For when I am weak, then I am strong.
2 CORINTHIANS 12:10 NKJV

God, thank You for giving me strength to do the things that seem hard. When I want to quit, help me to keep going. When I think I can't, help me to try anyway. Also help me be willing to ask others for help when I need it. Show me how to be a help and an encourager to my family when they are discouraged. Give me hope as I trust You to believe "I can!" Amen.

TALK ABOUT IT:

♥ Who in your family cheers you on the most?

♥ Who do you need to offer encouragement to more than you do?

"Deep in your hearts you know that every promise
of the LORD your God has come true.
Not a single one has failed!"
JOSHUA 23:14 NLT

Lord, sometimes things happen and we aren't able to keep
our promises. We mean to, we want to, but we fail. Thank
You that when You make a promise you always keep it.
I can always count on You to keep Your Word. Help me
to make promises I know I can keep. Show me how to be
trustworthy to those I make promises to. Amen.

TALK ABOUT IT:

- ♥ Have you made promises that you didn't keep?

- ♥ Do you need to ask forgiveness for not keeping those
  promises?

- ♥ Can you forgive those who have broken their promises
  to you?

Made in His Image

Then God said, "Let us make man in our image,
after our likeness. And let them have dominion over the fish
of the sea and over the birds of the heavens and over the
livestock and over all the earth and over every
creeping thing that creeps on the earth."
GENESIS 1:26 ESV

God, I want to be more and more like You. Just as I may
look like or act like my mom and dad, it's important that
I look and act like You. When others see me, I want them
to see Your love, Your mercy, Your grace, and Your peace.
Teach me Your Word that I may know You more and shine
Your light for others. Amen.

· · ♥ · ·

TALK ABOUT IT:

- ♥ Share a time when you saw God's goodness through
  someone else's actions.
- ♥ When do you think someone saw God in you?

God Is for You

*Your GOD is present among you, a strong Warrior there
to save you. Happy to have you back, he'll calm you with
his love and delight you with his songs.*
ZEPHANIAH 3:17 MSG

God, thank You for the people in my life that teach me and
show me how to grow. When I learned to do things for the
first time, someone taught me and cheered me on. As I
grow in my faith, I know that You are there with me, telling
me I can. When I fall down in my faith, You pick me up
and set me back on my feet. You gently nudge me to try
again. Amen.

· · ♥ · ·

TALK ABOUT IT:

♥ Think of a time when you wanted to give up, but
someone helped you succeed. Share that story with
your family.

Love Your Brothers and Sisters

There are six things the LORD hates—no, seven things
he detests: haughty eyes, a lying tongue, hands that kill the
innocent, a heart that plots evil, feet that race to do wrong,
a false witness who pours out lies, a person who
sows discord in a family.
PROVERBS 6:16-19 NLT

Lord, I want to love my brothers and sisters. When we
fight, when I am tempted to lash out, help me to think
before I speak. When I want to hit them, remind me that
is not Your way. I want to please You and show Your
goodness to my brothers and sisters. Amen.

TALK ABOUT IT:

- ♥ How does your family resolve conflict in a godly way?

- ♥ What helps you to show love to your family when
feelings are hurt?

Sin Remover

The next day John saw Jesus coming toward him.
John said, "Look, the Lamb of God, who takes
away the sin of the world!"
JOHN 1:29 NCV

Jesus, You came to take away my hurt and pain. When I do wrong, help me to be quick to ask for forgiveness from You and from others I have hurt. When I'm angry, I don't always want to ask for forgiveness, or offer forgiveness. Help me to have a soft heart, ready to give and receive forgiveness. Amen.

TALK ABOUT IT:

- ♥ Why is it hard sometimes to ask for forgiveness?
- ♥ Why is it hard to forgive someone who hurt you or made you mad?

The Greatest Trade Ever

For He made Him who knew no sin to be sin for us,
that we might become the righteousness of God in Him.
2 CORINTHIANS 5:21 NKJV

Jesus, thank You for making the greatest trade ever. All
You had to give was goodness and love, but You traded
something wonderful for something dark and ugly. You
took my sin so that I could be free. You gave me a clean
heart so that I could know God. Because of Your great
sacrifice, I can live forever. Help me to remember Your gift
to me and live each day remembering it. Amen.

· ∙ ♥ ∙ ·

TALK ABOUT IT:

- ♥ Would you ever trade something really good for
  something not so good? Why or why not?

- ♥ How can you show Jesus how thankful you are for
  what He was willing to give you?

Guard Your Lips

Those who control their tongue will have a long life;
opening your mouth can ruin everything.
PROVERBS 13:3 NLT

God, I have said things I shouldn't have said. Sometimes I speak before I think. I don't want to speak words that hurt others and hurt You. Help me to remember how much You love me, and how much You love my friends and family. I want to choose words that are pleasing to You—words that encourage others to know You. Amen.

TALK ABOUT IT:

♥ How can you control the words that come out of your mouth?

Opportunity and Open Doors

"I know your works. Behold, I have set before you an open door, which no one is able to shut. I know that you have but little power, and yet you have kept my word and have not denied my name."
REVELATION 3:8 ESV

Heavenly Father, thank You for the many blessings You have given to my family. Give my family wisdom to hear Your voice and follow You through each opportunity. As You open doors, help us to recognize Your provision and timing in each new adventure. Give us patience and grace to handle every change that comes our way. Amen.

· · 💜 · ·

TALK ABOUT IT:

- 💜 Are changes hard for you? For your family?
- 💜 What do you like about things staying the same?
- 💜 What is good about things changing?

Words of Grace

*Be gracious in your speech. The goal is to bring
out the best in others in a conversation,
not put them down, not cut them out.*
Colossians 4:6 MSG

Jesus, people who say mean things are not careful with
their words. I don't want to be one of those people. I want
to say good things about others. Even when the truth
needs to be spoken about something difficult, the Bible
shows that we can speak the truth in love. Give me wisdom
to speak words of grace. Help me to know when it's better
to keep my mouth shut and say nothing at all. Amen.

· · ♥ · ·

TALK ABOUT IT:

- ♥ How have good words helped you feel better about
  yourself or a situation?
- ♥ When did Jesus help you say the right thing?

Like Him

But the fruit of the [Holy] Spirit [the work which His presence within accomplishes] is love, joy (gladness), peace, patience (an even temper, forbearance), kindness, goodness (benevolence), faithfulness, gentleness (meekness, humility), self-control (self-restraint, continence). Against such things there is no law [that can bring a charge].
GALATIANS 5:22-23 AMP

God, we become like the people who are around us. That is why it's important to choose the right friends. And when we spend time with You, in prayer, reading Your Word, and praising You with singing, we grow in faith and become more like You. Teach me to be like You! Amen.

TALK ABOUT IT:

- ♥ What makes you feel close to God?
- ♥ What things do you say or do that makes others see God in you?

Power Up with Joy

Nehemiah said, "Go and enjoy good food and sweet drinks.
Send some to people who have none, because today is
a holy day to the Lord. Don't be sad, because the joy
of the LORD will make you strong."

NEHEMIAH 8:10 NCV

Lord, when I think about You—all You've done for me and for my family—I smile. You put a song in my heart. You fill me with good feelings. Even if I'm sad, I can think about Your goodness and how much You love me and feel better. You have given me so much. Thank You. Amen.

· · ♥ · ·

TALK ABOUT IT:

 ♥ When you are sad, what do you think about that brings a smile to your face?

 ♥ What has God done for you to make you smile?

123

The Spirit of Truth

However, when He, the Spirit of truth, has come,
He will guide you into all truth; for He will not speak
on His own authority, but whatever He hears
He will speak; and He will tell you things to come.
JOHN 16:13 NKJV

God, You want me to know the truth. Your truth shines bright, and in even the darkest places, I can see what is good and right. When others try to make me believe something that is not from You, I can know the truth because You speak to my heart. Your Word shines the light of truth into all the dark places and I am able to see what is real and what is not. Amen.

. . 💜 . .

TALK ABOUT IT:

- 💜 How can you know the truth?
- 💜 When you're unsure, who can you talk to about the truth?

Give Your All

Whatever you do, do well. For when you go to the grave,
there will be no work or planning or
knowledge or wisdom.
ECCLESIASTES 9:10 NLT

Jesus, I do things to please You, to please my parents, to please others. I do things because it makes me happy or simply because I want to do them. Whatever I do—for work or play—I want to do them well. As You live inside me, You help me to do what is good and right. Help me give it my all so that I can show others what it means to live my life for You. Amen.

TALK ABOUT IT:

- ♥ What things are hard for you?
- ♥ What things are easy for you?
- ♥ Do you ask for help from family? From Jesus?

Bubbling Over

*"The Lord is my strength and my song, and he has become
my salvation; this is my God, and I will praise him,
my father's God, and I will exalt him."*
EXODUS 15:2 ESV

Lord, the joy You give me just bubbles over. The more
I know You, the more I love You. You are everything
I need and more. When I ask, You answer. When You
give, I receive. When I am a little sad or discouraged, I
think about You and You bring me up again. Fill me to
overflowing with Your joy so I can share it with others
today. Amen.

TALK ABOUT IT:

- ♥ What sights, sounds, and thoughts remind you of the
  Lord's love for you?

- ♥ How do you feel when you're full of joy?

- ♥ How do you like to share His joy with your family?

Pour Out on Me

"I will pour out my Spirit on every kind of people:
Your sons will prophesy, also your daughters.
Your old men will dream, your young
men will see visions."
JOEL 2:28 MSG

Jesus, thank You for the gift of salvation so that I can know You personally. Because of this gift I willingly receive from You, You have promised to pour Your Spirit out on me. I can live each day following You, knowing that Your Spirit is with me, teaching me all things and preparing me for the future. Amen.

- - ♥ - -

TALK ABOUT IT:

♥ Identify the three names of the Trinity. What does each part mean to you?

Great is the Lord and highly to be praised;
and His greatness is [so vast and
deep as to be] unsearchable.
PSALM 145:3 AMP

Lord, You can never be praised enough. Even if I could spend an entire day celebrating You with singing, it wouldn't be enough time. Your goodness floods over me. Your mercy reaches deep into my heart and saves me. Keep my mind always on You, thinking about Your great love. You are more than enough for me. I want to take every opportunity to shout Your praise today. Amen.

• • ♥ • •

TALK ABOUT IT:

♥ What is a specific way that you praise God?

♥ When you think of God's great love what picture comes to your mind?

*Christ accepted you, so you should accept
each other, which will bring glory to God.*
ROMANS 15:7 NCV

Jesus, sometimes I am unsure of people who are different
from me. Sometimes they don't think like I do. Lots of
times they don't act like I do. They have a different sense of
humor or don't laugh at my jokes. Maybe they look or talk
differently. Remind me that I am different from others, too.
And You created all of us differently—I am good at some
things, but someone else is better at other things. When
we accept each other and share our strengths, we can do
more. Help me to accept others just as You have accepted
me. Amen.

TALK ABOUT IT:

- ♥ How are you different from other people in your
  family?
- ♥ What makes them special to you?

All Things are Possible with God

*But Jesus looked at them and said, "With men it
is impossible, but not with God; for with God
all things are possible."*
MARK 10:27 NKJV

God, I look to You for encouragement, safety, and peace.
The world does not have those things to offer. When I
take my eyes off of You, even for a second, things often
seem like they won't work out. But when I focus on You
and remember how much You love me, I know You have
everything under control. You provide me with a promise
that all things work together for my good (see Romans
8:28). Amen.

· · ♥ · ·

TALK ABOUT IT:

- ♥ When did God make the seemingly impossible,
  possible for your family?

- ♥ What is a problem you have today that you are
  trusting God to handle?

Angels at Your Service

Therefore, angels are only servants—spirits sent to care
for people who will inherit salvation.
HEBREWS 1:14 NLT

Heavenly Father, thank You for sending Your angels to keep me and my family safe. Please continue to send Your angels before us to clear the path we are to travel, or show us a different way. You are powerful and are in control of every step I take! Amen.

TALK ABOUT IT:

♥ Have you ever been caught in a storm away from home or found yourself lost? How did God make a way for you to return home safely?

No Matter What

Remove vexation from your heart, and put away pain from your body, for youth and the dawn of life are vanity.
ECCLESIASTES 11:10 ESV

Heavenly Father, shine the light of Your love into the dark places of my heart and show me the things that I need to work on—the things I say or do that aren't from You. Show me how I can be more like You. Show me how to make better choices that bring the goodness into my life. Thank You for loving me no matter what's in my heart, and for the promise of Your never-ending forgiveness that washes me clean. Amen.

· · 💙 · ·

TALK ABOUT IT:

💜 How can you know if you have some dark places in your heart that are creeping in?

A Daily Choice

"Call me and I'll answer, be at your side in bad times;
I'll rescue you, then throw you a party. I'll give you
a long life, give you a long drink of salvation!"
PSALM 91:16 MSG

Lord, You are my helper and my friend. Some days become very busy, and I feel like I am squeezing You into my day. I don't want to only give You a tiny slice of my life. You gave Your all, and so I give all of me. Give me a hunger to be with You just as I am hungry to eat food each day. Amen.

TALK ABOUT IT:

- ♥ Why do you think it is important to spend time with the Lord?

- ♥ How can you choose to put your friendship with the Lord first each day?

To Value Wisdom

Skillful and godly Wisdom is more precious than rubies;
and nothing you can wish for is to be compared to her.
Length of days is in her right hand, and in her left
hand are riches and honor.
PROVERBS 3:15-16 AMP

Lord, I need Your wisdom. Help me to recognize what You want rather than what I want. Remind me that Your way is the best way. I don't want to confuse the situation, but instead follow Your leadership. Let me see Your wisdom and choose to walk in it every single day. Amen.

• • 💜 • •

TALK ABOUT IT:

💜 Would you rather try to figure out things on your own or rely on someone else to tell you what to do?

💜 Tell about a time that you made a *wrong* decision and what you learned from it.

All Is Well

*Children, obey your parents as the Lord wants, because this
is the right thing to do. The command says, "Honor your
father and mother." This is the first command that has a
promise with it—"Then everything will be well with you,
and you will have a long life on the earth."*
EPHESIANS 6:1–3 NCV

Heavenly Father, thank You for the many gifts You've
given me. As I honor and obey my parents, I have Your
promise of a long life—an eternal life! I choose each day to
obey them and obey Your Word. Give me a real desire to
do what is right. As I grow to know You more, teach me to
hear and obey You also. Amen.

TALK ABOUT IT:

- Why do you think we sometimes disobey?
- In obeying your parents, how does that help you learn
  to obey God?

In Your Footsteps

*"For by me your days will be multiplied,
and years of life will be added to you."*
PROVERBS 9:11 NKJV

Jesus, You are leading me on the path You have chosen
for my life. I never have to walk alone. I will walk in Your
footsteps as You point the way. Help me to listen closely to
Your voice. If I am busy or distracted, remind me to look
up and get back on the path where I belong. As I follow
You, I know I will always be in the right place at the right
time. Amen.

TALK ABOUT IT:

- ♥ Jesus loves you and has given you a purpose. What do
  you think that purpose might be?

- ♥ What are some ways you can learn your purpose?

Forever Is Now

"Today I have given you the choice between life and death, between blessings and curses. Now I call on heaven and earth to witness the choice you make. Oh, that you would choose life, so that you and your descendants might live!"
DEUTERONOMY 30:19 NLT

Heavenly Father, You have given me a choice, and I choose life. It's not just life after death—but the beginning of forever—a life with You that has no end. My forever started the moment I asked You into my heart. Help me to make good choices every day—choices that please You and bring blessing to my family. Amen.

TALK ABOUT IT:

♥ How do you feel when you've made a good choice?

♥ When you realize you've made a mistake, what is the best thing to do?

*"You shall walk in all the way that the LORD your God
has commanded you, that you may live, and that it may
go well with you, and that you may live long in
the land that you shall possess."*
DEUTERONOMY 5:33 ESV

God, since I've given my life to You, it no longer belongs
to me. I want to please You in all I say and all I do. Help me
to remember that I belong to You. You hold my life in Your
hands. Give me wise leaders to help me grow in my faith.
Give me role models that point me to You and Your will for
my life. Give me ears to hear and a heart to do all that You
have dreamed for me. Amen.

· · 💙 · ·

TALK ABOUT IT:

💙 What do you think might be God's dream for you?

138

Seeds of Goodness

These are the words in my mouth; these are what I chew on and pray. Accept them when I place them on the morning altar, O God, my Altar-Rock, God, Priest-of-My-Altar.
PSALM 19:14 MSG

Jesus, what I say and do matters. Sometimes I say words I don't mean and later regret. As I think on good things, seeds of goodness bring good things to my lips. Fill my spirit with Your goodness as I study and pray. Help me to consider my words by thinking about what You would say before I open my mouth. Amen.

· · ♥ · ·

TALK ABOUT IT:

- ♥ When someone does something to upset you, how do you respond?
- ♥ How can you let seeds of goodness grow in your heart?

*If I am detained, you may know how people ought
to conduct themselves in the household of God,
which is the church of the living God, the pillar and
stay (the prop and support) of the Truth.*
1 TIMOTHY 3:15 AMP

Lord, thank You for my church family. I pray You give us
eyes to see the talents You have given each of us. Show
us how we can see our differences as strengths that can
help one another so that we can work together in pointing
others to You. Open our hearts and fill us with love and
compassion that we may really care about one another—
like You care for each of us. Amen.

· · 💜 · ·

TALK ABOUT IT:

💜 What is your favorite thing about your church?

Do not be interested only in your own life,
but be interested in the lives of others.
PHILIPPIANS 2:4 NCV

Heavenly Father, the way I choose to behave each day either adds to or takes away from the lives of others. When I am grouchy, short-tempered, and rude to others, it can take the life out of them like a balloon that loses air. When I am helpful, loving, and giving it can fill them up with good things. Help me to be a balloon filler, not a deflater. Amen.

TALK ABOUT IT:

♥ Who do you know that is a good balloon filler?

Let the Whole World Know

Declare His glory among the nations,
His wonders among all peoples.
PSALM 96:3 NKJV

Jesus, I pray others see the light of Your goodness in our family. They watch us when we don't realize it. May they see us love each other as we go through our day. Help us to be kind to one another in all we say and do. Help us choose peace and compassion. Show us opportunities to be generous and thoughtful to our neighbors. Remind us to show simple acts of kindness today. Amen.

TALK ABOUT IT:

- ♥ What can you do today or tomorrow to let Christ shine in you?

- ♥ When has the Lord given you opportunities to show His love to others?

Make Our Home a Place of Prayer

"For where two or three gather together as my followers,
I am there among them."
MATTHEW 18:20 NLT

Jesus, You promised Your followers that when we get
together, You are with us. Let us spend time together
in prayer as a family. As we spend time with You and
with each other, we will grow in faith and in love for one
another. When my family member hurts, help me to show
love and compassion and a willingness to pray for them.
Show me how to pray for our family for today and for our
future. Amen.

TALK ABOUT IT:

♥ When was the last time you prayed for someone in
your family?

♥ Do you have something you want your family to pray
with you about now?

Weave Our Hearts Together

*And they devoted themselves to the apostles'
teaching and the fellowship, to the breaking
of bread and the prayers.*
ACTS 2:42 ESV

Lord, bring our family closer together. Because we know
each other so well, we know how to help or hurt each other.
When we're tempted to treat each other badly, gently
remind us that we are here to share Your love with one
another. Strengthen us to face the challenges we have every
day. No matter what we come against, help us to depend on
You and on each other to carry us through. Amen.

TALK ABOUT IT:

♥ How has someone in your family shown you love this
week?

God's Great Love

They'll get to know me by being kindly forgiven,
with the slate of their sins forever wiped clean.
HEBREWS 8:12 MSG

God, as I get to know You, I love You even more! It makes me want to please You and do what is right in Your sight. Your great love for me makes me want to share that love with others. I want others to know You and experience who You are to me and who You can be to them. Help me show others Your great love at work in me. Amen.

TALK ABOUT IT:

- ♥ When have you seen God's great love in others?
- ♥ What can you do to show others in your family His love?

Life Giver

*The thief comes only in order to steal and kill and destroy.
I came that they may have and enjoy life, and have it in
abundance (to the full, till it overflows).*
JOHN 10:10 AMP

Jesus, I am so thankful to know You and have a personal
relationship with You. You add to my life and never
subtract from it. You give, give, give. Help me to forgive
those who take away from my life. Thank You for family
that loves me and wants me to know You more. Thank You
for helping me to grow closer to You as I live each day with
them. Amen.

• • 💚 • •

TALK ABOUT IT:

- 💜 How does Jesus add to your life?
- 💜 How has your family added to your life?

Goodbye to Sin

*You will have mercy on us again; you will conquer
our sins. You will throw away all our sins into
the deepest part of the sea.*
MICAH 7:19 NCV

Heavenly Father, when I sin, help me to be quick to ask for
forgiveness. Thank You for always loving and forgiving me.
Remind me that You don't remember my sin after You've
forgiven me. You won't bring it up to me again. Thank You
for helping me as I accept the consequences for my actions
after I truly repent for the wrong I have done. Amen.

· · ♥ · ·

TALK ABOUT IT:
- ♥ Why is it hard to say you're sorry?
- ♥ Why does it hurt to accept the consequences of your sin?

One afternoon about three o'clock, he had a vision in which
he saw an angel of God coming toward him. "Cornelius!"
the angel said. Cornelius stared at him in terror.
"What is it, sir?" he asked the angel. And the angel replied,
"Your prayers and gifts to the poor have been
received by God as an offering!"
ACTS 10:3-4 NLT

Lord, help me to listen as I pray. Remind me that the
answers to the questions I ask of You can come from
others. You have given wisdom to my family and
sometimes Your wisdom can come out of their hearts and
mouths. Help me to have an open heart when You speak to
me. Amen.

TALK ABOUT IT:

- ♥ When has someone else helped you understand the
  answer to a question you asked the Lord?

- ♥ How do you know God hears your prayers?

What You Say Matters

Death and life are in the power of the tongue,
and those who love it will eat its fruit.
PROVERBS 18:21 NKJV

God, You created the universe and the whole world with
Your words. Your words have power. You created me in
Your image, with power in my words. My words—good or
bad—can encourage others or tear them down. Help me to
be careful with my words. I want to honor You with all that
comes out of my mouth. Help me to understand that what I
say really does matter. Amen.

TALK ABOUT IT:

- ♥ Have you ever said something—even as a joke—that
  you wish you could take back?

- ♥ How important is it to consider your words before you
  say them?

- ♥ What are some words you like to hear said to you?

For His Very Best

*Thus says the L*ORD*, your Redeemer, the Holy One of Israel:*
*"I am the L*ORD *your God, who teaches you to profit,*
who leads you in the way you should go."
ISAIAH 48:17 ESV

Heavenly Father, whatever I need, You show me the best way
to meet that need. You provide for me and for my family.
You give us Your very best. Give us wisdom and grace to
do things Your way. Sometimes we want things to happen
faster—so give us patience as we wait on You to make things
happen according to Your plan. Help us to trust and wait on
You. Amen.

TALK ABOUT IT:

♥ Why does God want His best for you?

♥ Do you believe your family wants what is best for you?

Put On the Armor of God

Is not this the God who armed me well,
then aimed me in the right direction?
2 SAMUEL 22:33 MSG

Heavenly Father, we put on the full armor of God today starting with the shoes of the Gospel of peace so we may walk in Your peace. We put on the belt of truth so that we may live the truth found in the Bible. We guard our hearts with the breastplate of righteousness and protect our minds, wills, and emotions with the helmet of salvation. We stand firm with the shield of faith before us and the sword of the Spirit, the Bible. Guide us and protect us as we go out into the world today and keep us in all our ways. Amen.

• • ♥ • •

TALK ABOUT IT:

♥ Discuss each of the different pieces of armor (see Ephesians 6:10-20).

Bold Praise

And in that day you will say, Give thanks to the Lord,
call upon His name and by means of His name
[in solemn entreaty]; declare and make known
His deeds among the peoples of the earth,
proclaim that His name is exalted!
ISAIAH 12:4 AMP

Lord, You have given me so much. Forgive me for my silence in response to the little gifts and miraculous works You've done for me and my family. Starting today I will tell the world of Your goodness. I will not be quiet! I will open my mouth to tell others how You shower me with Your love and mercy. Thank You! Amen.

· · 💛 · ·

TALK ABOUT IT:

- 💜 When was the last time you told someone something good about God?
- 💜 How can you become bolder in telling His story to others?

So Much Love

"God loved the world so much that he gave his one
and only Son so that whoever believes in him
may not be lost, but have eternal life."
JOHN 3:16 NCV

God, when we think of gifts, we usually think of objects
that are wrapped in a package. The way I show love to my
family—the way I treat them—can be a gift to them. Help
me to give the gifts of mercy, grace, and understanding.
Help me to show patience and kindness. Remind me that
there are things in my life that are more important than
myself. Amen.

TALK ABOUT IT:

♥ Name some of the gifts you've received from family
lately that you can't hold in your hands.

♥ What gifts can you give to family each day? To
friends? To those you don't know?

"But seek first the kingdom of God and His righteousness, and all these things shall be added to you."
MATTHEW 6:33 NKJV

God, our family is so busy. We all have many things we need to do. In the middle of our busy schedules, help us to remember that our first love is You! You are the foundation of our home and hearts. Forgive us when we lose sight of where we've been, how far we've come, and to whom we belong. May we continually make You the center of all we do. Amen.

TALK ABOUT IT:

- How do you feel when you realize you forgot to include God in a part of your day?
- What helps you keep Him at the center of all you do?

154

Proof of Your Love

"If you love me, obey my commandments."
JOHN 14:15 NLT

Heavenly Father, You call me Your chosen child. I know
You love me. One way I can show You how much I love
You is to follow Your commandments. Teach me Your
Word that I may obey You. I want You to be pleased with
my choices each day. When I struggle to make the right
choice—Yours instead of mine—help me to choose to obey
You. Amen.

. . ♥ . .

TALK ABOUT IT:

- ♥ What choices have you made that show you love God?
- ♥ How does obeying your parents show God how much
  you love Him and them?

155

Innovative Ideas

The plans of the diligent lead surely to abundance,
but everyone who is hasty comes only to poverty.
PROVERBS 21:5 ESV

God, You are the Creator of all. If it exists, You created it.
You knew every idea before it was thought by anyone. You
understood every invention before a human dreamed it
up. You gave talents to each one of us. Please help us to
be creative with the dream You put into each of our hearts.
Bring those ideas to the surface and show us what You
would have us to do with them. Amen.

TALK ABOUT IT:

♥ What special gift do you see in each of your family
members?

♥ What talent do you see that God has put in you?

156

Count on Jesus

For Jesus doesn't change—yesterday, today,
tomorrow, he's always totally himself.
HEBREWS 13:8 MSG

Jesus, things in my world change. Sometimes that's good and sometimes it's not. When I expect something to happen or be a certain way, and it doesn't turn out that way, I can be disappointed or even hurt. Thank You for being someone I can always count on. It gives me courage and strength to know that You never change. When the Bible makes a promise, I know I can believe it. Thank You for always being there for me—unchanging and consistent in my life. Amen.

TALK ABOUT IT:

- ♥ Can your family count on you? Why or why not?
- ♥ How does it make you feel to know that Jesus doesn't change?
- ♥ Who, besides Jesus, do you know you can count on?

Confidence

Commit your way to the Lord [roll and repose each
care of your load on Him]; trust (lean on,
rely on, and be confident) also in Him
and He will bring it to pass.
PSALM 37:5 AMP

Lord, I want to believe I can do all things. Your strength
within me helps me to become who You created me to
be. Help me to stand up to the pressure others place on
me. I don't have to do it on my own. You are with me—You
are my confidence! You give me strength to face today's
challenges. I remind myself of all the things that You have
done for me. With You at my side and in my heart—I know
I can! Amen.

TALK ABOUT IT:

♥ When you are pushed outside of your comfort zone,
how do you respond?

When It Seems Unfair

But he said to me, "My grace is enough for you.
When you are weak, my power is made perfect in you."
So I am very happy to brag about my weaknesses.
Then Christ's power can live in me.
2 CORINTHIANS 12:9 NCV

God, there are things that happen that seem so unfair. Sometimes it happens to others; sometimes to me, but either way I don't like it. I want to take matters in my own hands and try to work it out. I want to explain when others can't or won't listen. You promised Your grace is enough. Cover my heart with peace. Help me to trust You and trust my family even when I don't understand. Amen.

· · 💜 · ·

TALK ABOUT IT:

💜 How do you respond when things feel unfair?

💜 How does God want you to respond?

Thanks for Grace

You therefore, my son,
be strong in the grace that is in Christ Jesus.
2 TIMOTHY 2:1 NKJV

Lord, today I am thankful for my family and the faith
we share. You loved us from the beginning and offered
salvation to save us from a lost world. It's nothing we've
done to deserve Your saving grace. We can't buy it or earn
it through good deeds. You gave it freely to each of us, and
it's up to us to accept it. Today I receive Your gift of favor
and blessing—Your grace. Thank You for showering Your
favor and love on my life and my family. Please bless each
family member today! Amen.

. . 💚 . .

TALK ABOUT IT:

- 💜 What can you do to show God's favor and blessing
  (grace) to each family member?
- 💜 How does your family show God's grace to you?

Hope in the Lord

But those who trust in the LORD will find new strength.
They will soar high on wings like eagles. They will run
and not grow weary. They will walk and not faint.
ISAIAH 40:31 NLT

Lord, even the strongest and most fit athletes grow tired.
My life in You is not just about the physical—what I see,
touch, taste, hear, and feel—but includes the spiritual.
When I am tired, Lord, remind me that I can look to You for
strength. Encourage me and tell me how I can keep going,
when I feel like I can't. Give me words of encouragement
for others as well. My hope is in You. Amen.

TALK ABOUT IT:

- ♥ What reminds you to hope in the Lord? A scripture, a
  song, a word from a friend?
- ♥ When you want to quit, who helps you keep going?

With Thanksgiving

Give thanks to the God of heaven,
for his steadfast love endures forever.
PSALM 136:26 ESV

Heavenly Father, today we just want to thank You. You are good. You created us and all that we are. Our prayer times are not about getting something from You, but instead just spending a few minutes telling You how much we love You, honor You, and appreciate You! Your love for us never stops. Even when we think we have exceeded all the grace that You could possibly give, You give us more. From morning to night, day after day, You always show us Your love. Thank You for being the loving, giving Father we need each day. Amen.

TALK ABOUT IT:

♥ Tell about a time when you felt loved very much, by God or by a family member.

For His Name's Sake

Not for our sake, God, no, not for our sake, but for your name's sake, show your glory. Do it on account of your merciful love, do it on account of your faithful ways.
PSALM 115:1 MSG

God, not for our sake, but for Your name's sake, show Your glory. Do it because of Your merciful love and Your faithful ways. Do it so no one can say, "Where now, oh where is their God?" We put our trust in You. You are faithful, O God, to remember us and bless us, and bless our families. We bless You now, we bless You always! Hallelujah! (See Psalm 115.) Amen.

· ∘ ♥ ∘ ·

TALK ABOUT IT:

♥ Why do you think God wants to bless you and your family?

♥ What do His blessings in your life say to other people?

For His Loving-Kindness

O give thanks to the Lord, for He is good;
for His mercy and loving-kindness endure forever.
PSALM 136:1 AMP

Lord, thank You for Your mercy and loving-kindness.
You alone do great wonders that demonstrate Your good
nature. You made the heavens and stretched out the earth
upon the waters. You made the sun to rule over the day,
the moon and stars to rule by night. You remembered us
and imprinted us on Your heart. You rescued us from our
enemies, for Your mercy and loving-kindness are forever
and ever. (See Psalm 136.) Amen.

. . 💛 . .

TALK ABOUT IT:

- 💛 What does it mean for God to imprint you upon His
  heart?

- 💛 What does that say about how much He loves you?

- 💛 How can you say thank You to God?

The Reason for Worship

*I will sing to the LORD all my life; I will sing praises
to my God as long as I live. May my thoughts
please him; I am happy in the LORD.*
PSALM 104:33-34 NCV

Lord, You built the earth on its foundations so it can never
be moved. You covered the earth with oceans; the water
was above the mountains. But at Your command, the water
rushed away. The earth is full of the things You made. The
earth is full of Your riches. I will sing to You, Lord, all my
life. I want my thoughts to please You; I am happy in the
Lord. Amen.

· · ♥ · ·

TALK ABOUT IT:

♥ When you read the Bible, you discover God thought
of everything and put it into its place. Talk about the
things God made and how that gives you reason to
praise Him.

Look to Your Shepherd

The LORD is my shepherd; I shall not want. He makes me to lie down in green pastures; He leads me beside the still waters. He restores my soul; He leads me in the paths of righteousness for His name's sake.

PSALM 23:1–3 NKJV

Lord, You take great care of me, like a shepherd cares for his sheep. Your eyes are always on me. Never let me wander away and become lost. I pray You always come after me if I stray from You. Amen.

· · 💜 · ·

TALK ABOUT IT:

💜 Have you ever become distracted and suddenly found yourself lost from your family in a crowded place? How did that feel?

*Devote yourselves to prayer with an
alert mind and a thankful heart.*
COLOSSIANS 4:2 NLT

Heavenly Father, I want to pray hard for others who don't
know You. Please give me the opportunity to tell them
about You. And when my turn comes to share You with
them, I want to be ready, prayed up, and overflowing with
Your words for them. Amen.

TALK ABOUT IT:

♥ If you go a few days without praying or talking to God,
what do you feel like? Does it affect your attitude?
Your heart?

♥ How does it feel to be prayed up?

For the Sour Heart

See to it that no one fails to obtain the grace of God;
that no "root of bitterness" springs up and causes trouble,
and by it many become defiled.
HEBREWS 12:15 ESV

God, when I am angry, hurt, scared, and feeling alone, my
heart can turn sour like milk when it's gone bad. A sour
heart hurts me and hurts those I love. No one wants to be
around me because my attitude can stink. Please speak
to my heart when I'm in that sour place. Help me to pour
out all the bitterness. Rinse me with forgiveness and fill
me with Your love. Heal me so that I may become a sweet
smell to You and to others. Amen.

TALK ABOUT IT:

- ♥ Has anyone in your family had a sour heart at times?
  Have you?
- ♥ How does sourness make you feel?

Name-Calling

"I'm telling you that anyone who is so much as angry with a brother or sister is guilty of murder. Carelessly call a brother 'idiot!' and you just might find yourself hauled into court. Thoughtlessly yell 'stupid!' at a sister and you are on the brink of hellfire. The simple moral fact is that words kill."
MATTHEW 5:22 MSG

God, it hurts my feelings when people call me names. But when that happens, help me not to be mean back. Then remind me of the good names You have called me. I am Your *treasured possession*, and Your *masterpiece* crafted by Your hand. I am *loved* beyond measure. I belong to You. You have called me Your own child. Amen.

· · ♥ · ·

TALK ABOUT IT:

♥ What are some good names you call your family members?

♥ What other good names can you think of that God has called you?

Imagine the Power

*And if the Spirit of Him Who raised up Jesus from the dead
dwells in you, [then] He Who raised up Christ Jesus from
the dead will also restore to life your mortal (short-lived,
perishable) bodies through His Spirit Who dwells in you.*
ROMANS 8:11 AMP

Jesus, sometimes I feel powerless and too small to help.
Then I remember that the Bible says Your Spirit—Your
power—lives inside of me. I have all the power I need. I can
do all things because of Christ living in me. I can ask for
help from You and from others. I can't do everything on my
own. But with You, all things are possible. Amen.

TALK ABOUT IT:

- What is one thing you struggle to do?
- Have you asked God to help you do it in His power?

Power in His Name

"You must not use the name of the LORD your God thoughtlessly; the LORD will punish anyone who misuses his name."
EXODUS 20:7 NCV

Jesus, Your name is powerful. It hurts Your heart to hear people use Your name to curse. In our home, we honor Your name and use it to bring You glory. May we always speak Your name with love. When others misuse Your name, give us wisdom in how to respond in love, but also in a way that lets them know that Your name is special to us. We cherish Your name—the name above all other names. Amen.

TALK ABOUT IT:

- ♥ When you heard someone misuse the name of the Lord, how did you respond?
- ♥ How will you respond in the future?

Understanding the Bible

*[Jesus] answered and said, "It is written, 'Man shall not
live by bread alone, but by every word that
proceeds from the mouth of God.'"*
MATTHEW 4:4 NKJV

God, thank You for the Bible. Your Word is true and does
not change. You breathed Your Word into the hearts of
men, who wrote it down. Give me understanding as I read
it. It shows me how to live my life in a way that will please
You. It gives me a picture of who You are, what You've
done, and will do. It gives me hope for my future. Give me
a hunger to read the Bible, to learn from it, and to apply it
to my life today. Amen.

· · 💜 · ·

TALK ABOUT IT:

💜 What is one thing you have learned from a Bible story
or verse?

Dead to Sin

Since we have died to sin,
how can we continue to live in it?
ROMANS 6:2 NLT

Jesus, through Your death, burial, and resurrection, You paid the price and broke the hold that sin had on me. I have received You as my Lord and Savior, and now I can live my life free from sin. Help me to choose Your way, to live in freedom. When I stumble or fail, help me to quickly repent. Asking for forgiveness keeps me close to You! Amen.

TALK ABOUT IT:

- ♥ How do you feel in your heart when you've sinned?
- ♥ When you have sinned, what is the first thing you should do?

The Art of Giving

Each one must give as he has decided in his heart,
not reluctantly or under compulsion,
for God loves a cheerful giver.
2 CORINTHIANS 9:7 ESV

God, I want to be a cheerful giver. Sometimes I have things I want to hold on to and not share with others. The Bible tells us that everything comes from You. All we have as a family, all that I call mine, You gave to me. You give and give to those You love every day. Teach me to have an open heart to give to others. Help me to become a cheerful giver! Amen.

• ● ♥ ● •

TALK ABOUT IT:

- ♥ When have you seen someone receive something they really wanted or needed? How did you feel in that moment?

- ♥ What are some things you think God might have you give?

Shining as the Stars

Be energetic in your life of salvation, reverent and sensitive before God. That energy is God's energy, an energy deep within you, God himself willing and working at what will give him the most pleasure.
PHILIPPIANS 2:12–13 MSG

Lord, I want to live my life in a way that is pleasing to You. When I obey my parents, it pleases You. When I choose what is good and right, it pleases You. When I look to the heavens and see the stars shining bright, I want to be a light for the world to see. Help me to live my life in a way that I shine bright and bring You glory that the world can see You in me. Amen.

• • ♥ • •

TALK ABOUT IT:

♥ Tell about a time when you saw the light of God in the choices of a family member.

*Brethren, [with all] my heart's desire and goodwill for
[Israel], I long and pray to God that they may be saved.*
ROMANS 10:1 AMP

Jesus, You love every person on the earth and want them
to believe in You. Today I pray for those who don't know
You. I pray that their hearts become open and ready to
receive You. If I meet someone who doesn't know You,
please speak through me to encourage them to know You.
I pray that when You knock on their heart's door, that they
will hear You knocking and invite You in. Then You will
hug them tight and show them love like they've never
known before. Amen.

• • 💚 • •

TALK ABOUT IT:

💜 Do you know someone who doesn't know Jesus? Take
time now with your family to pray for that person by
name.

To Overflow with Hope

I pray that the God who gives hope will fill you with much joy and peace while you trust in him. Then your hope will overflow by the power of the Holy Spirit.
ROMANS 15:13 NCV

God, there are a lot of negative people in the world who see the darkness instead of the light. They say things opposite to Your Word. They refuse to believe Your promises. Fill me with the hope of Christ so I can share that hope. Let me help others to hope when they think they have no hope. Let them see Your hope in me! Amen.

TALK ABOUT IT:

♥ What do others say or do to help you experience hope?

♥ How can you give the hope of Christ to others?

Show Me What You've Put in My Heart

"Eye has not seen, nor ear heard, nor have entered into the heart of man the things which God has prepared for those who love Him." But God has revealed them to us through His Spirit. For the Spirit searches all things, yes, the deep things of God.
1 CORINTHIANS 2:9-10 NKJV

Heavenly Father, You have amazing plans for my life. You placed Your purpose deep within my heart. Each day is an adventure with You. Help me to listen to You and follow Your instruction so that I live the way You want me to. When people say I can't do something, remind me that You said that with Your help, I can do *anything*! Amen.

TALK ABOUT IT:

♥ How does it make you feel to know God believes in you?

Undeserved Favor and Blessing

For the grace of God (His unmerited favor and blessing)
has come forward (appeared) for the deliverance from
sin and the eternal salvation for all mankind.
TITUS 2:11 AMP

God, my family is a great gift. The love we share, the
hope we have together in You is special. Just as You
give me good things for no other reason than that You
love me, I want to give good things to those I love.
Help me to show compassion, love, joy, and patience—
especially when I think they don't deserve it—just as You
have loved me. Amen.

· · 🩷 · ·

TALK ABOUT IT:

🩷 How can you bless a family member today? What
words would you use? What actions could you take?

So let's not get tired of doing what is good.
At just the right time we will reap a harvest
of blessing if we don't give up.
GALATIANS 6:9 NLT

Jesus, You are our hope. You know each one in our family—
our strengths and our weaknesses. Things in life can
come like a big wave and try to take us down. Help us to
remember no matter how big the wave, it can never drown
out our cries of help to You. Our prayers are never lost. You
always hear us. When difficulty comes to discourage and
destroy us, we will stay afloat because nothing can keep us
from Your love that saves us. Amen.

TALK ABOUT IT:

- ♥ What helps you keep going when you want to quit?
- ♥ How do you encourage each other to believe?

Learning to Wait

But let him ask in faith, with no doubting,
for the one who doubts is like a wave of the sea
that is driven and tossed by the wind.
JAMES 1:6 ESV

Jesus, I want to believe Your promise that when I ask,
I will receive. But it's the waiting that is hard. Once I've
prayed and believed, sometimes time goes on and I begin
to doubt. I want to trust You, to believe You, and do things
Your way. Give me strength and patience to trust You while
I wait. Help me to believe You heard me and that You're
working behind the scenes to show me Your undeniable
love. Amen.

• • 💚 • •

TALK ABOUT IT:

♥ Why is it hard to trust when you don't see action?

♥ What helps you to believe God is at work even when
you can't see it?

Live Connected

*"You're blessed when you get your inside world—
your mind and heart—put right. Then you can see
God in the outside world."*
MATTHEW 5:8 MSG

Heavenly Father, I don't want to miss a single day of Your
goodness. Show me how to live each moment connected to
Your power and presence. Show me how to work with You
to accomplish the great purpose You've given me. Teach me
who You are and lead me daily as I walk with You. Amen.

· · 💜 · ·

TALK ABOUT IT:

💜 How can you connect with God today?

Do What's Right

*So whoever knows the right thing to do
and fails to do it, for him it is sin.*
JAMES 4:17 ESV

Jesus, doing wrong is sin, but not doing what's right is
also sin. It takes courage to stand up for what's right. It
might mean being the only person to choose the right
thing when everyone else goes the wrong way. Give me the
strength to do what is right no matter what other people
say. Speak to my heart and show me how to choose Your
way—the right way. Amen.

TALK ABOUT IT:

♥ When was a time when you didn't speak up for what
was right? How did you feel?

♥ Tell about a time you did the right thing. How did you
feel?

Thank You for Loving Us

No one has greater love [no one has shown stronger affection] than to lay down (give up) his own life for his friends.
JOHN 15:13 AMP

God, we can always count on You to love us unconditionally. No matter what we do, or don't do, You will never stop loving us. You never go back on Your promises to us. You are always faithful to be there when we need You. We can rest in You and trust that You will never fail! Your love for our family is a forever love! Amen.

· · ♥ · ·

TALK ABOUT IT:

♥ What does it mean to love unconditionally?

♥ Do you ever put conditions on loving someone? How or why?

Right Side Out Again

*Now may the Lord direct your hearts into the love
of God and into the patience of Christ.*
2 THESSALONIANS 3:5 NKJV

Lord, before I knew You, I was wrong side out, like when I turn my clothes inside out when I take them off. My body told me what to think and feel through my five senses. When I received You as my Savior, You turned me right side out. You created me to live first by my spirit, following You. You made my spirit clean and new. Help me learn to be Spirit-led. Lead and guide me and show me Your ways that I may become more like You. Amen.

TALK ABOUT IT:

♥ How does living with your Spirit in charge change what your body and soul should do?

"If I were you, I would go to God and present my case to him. He does great things too marvelous to understand. He performs countless miracles."

JOB 5:8–9 NLT

God, there are times I feel alone, like no one will understand me or what I am feeling. Help me to remember that the enemy of my soul, the devil, wants to separate me from all who know and love me. Instead of hiding away and feeling sorry for myself, give me courage to share my feelings with You and with my family. The best way to break those harmful lies is to tell You and let You show me that You understand. I'm not alone. Amen.

TALK ABOUT IT:

- ♥ Why do you think we want to be alone when we're sad?
- ♥ How do you feel after you share your feelings with someone you trust?

Scripture Index

Pressed for Time? Get These 3-Minute Pick-Me-Ups!

Too Blessed to be Stressed: 3-Minute Devotions for Women by **Deb Coty**

Women will find the spiritual pick-me-up they desire in *Too Blessed to Be Stressed: 3-Minute Devotions for Women*. 180 uplifting readings from bestselling author Debora M. Coty pack a powerful dose of comfort, encouragement, humor, and inspiration into just-right-sized readings for women on the go.

Paperback / 978-1-63409-569-3 / $4.99

Daily Wisdom: 3-Minute Devotions for Women
Daily Wisdom for Women has touched the lives of more than three quarters of a million readers since its release nearly two decades ago. Now in a great "3-Minute Devotions" edition, this devotional will continue to encourage new generations of women as they seek the true wisdom only found in God's Word.

Paperback / 978-1-63409-689-8 / $4.99

Find These and More from Barbour Books
at Your Favorite Bookstore
www.barbourbooks.com

BARBOUR
PUBLISHING